TITLE:	OLD WOMAN AT PLAY
AUTHOR:	Adele Wiseman
PUBLISHERS:	Clarke, Irwin & Co. Ltd. 791 St. Clair Ave. West Toronto, Ontario, Canada M6C 1B8
SUBJECT:	Non-Fiction. The author explores her mother's life and art as a dollmaker
RIGHTS AVAILABLE:	U.S., U.K., foreign language, film and T.V.
FORMAT:	160 pages, 8 x 8 hardback
PUB. DATE	1978
PRICE:	$14.95 Canadian
CONTACT:	Carolyn Dodds Subsidiary Rights Clarke, Irwin & Co. Ltd.

Old Woman at Play

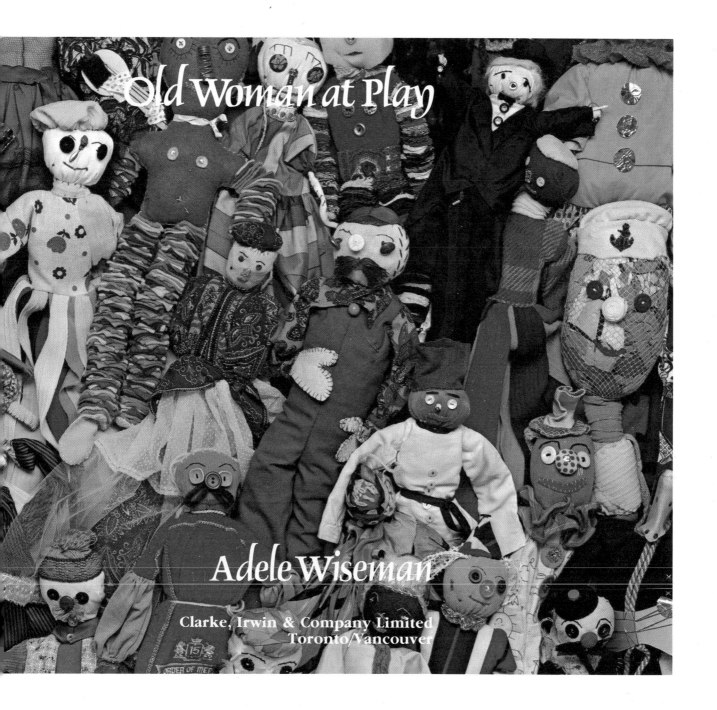

Old Woman at Play

Adele Wiseman

Clarke, Irwin & Company Limited
Toronto/Vancouver

The writer wishes to thank the
Canada Council Explorations
Program for a grant which helped
enable her to work on this book.

The Publisher wishes to
acknowledge the generous
assistance of the Multicultural
Program of the Government of
Canada towards the publication of
this book.

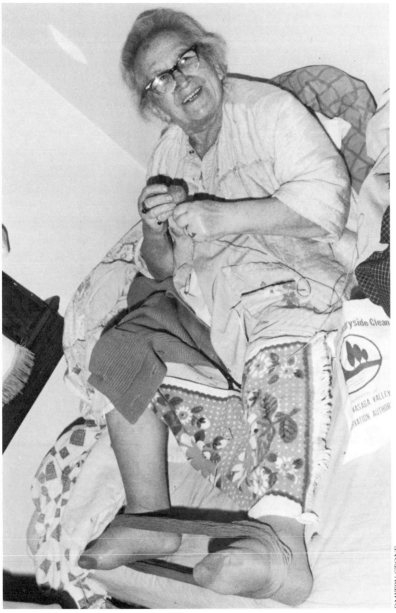

This book is for her children
and their spouses,
for her grandchildren:
Arnold Harvey Alan Wiseman,
Jacques Joseph Distler,
Vivian Bliss Distler,
Tamara Risa Esther Bliss Stone,
and for all the other children and
grandchildren whom she has
made and will yet make her own.

Old Woman at Play

By four o'clock in the morning my mother begins to feel sleepy. She stabs her needle in and out, anchoring it on the breast of her dress. She gathers up thimble, scissors, and scraps of material. She folds the Yiddish paper, and clicks off the ancient mantel radio which has been set at the all-night classical music program. She washes, sinks her upper dentures, and donning one of her delicately flowered, amply gathered, frilled, sleeveless and scoop-necked nightgowns, she turns out lights and feels her way into bed. She lies quietly, on her side, curled up and invisible, except for a wisp or so of gray hair if you look closely enough, a plump little mound under the covers, with somewhere, a breathing hole.

Around noon, her long, fine nose will appear first from under the stirring hillock. Though normally awakened instantly by any sound, she will take care now to get up slowly, so as not to disturb her "pressure," and to avoid the giddiness and the heavy head. She puts on her glasses first thing, reminding herself to clean them later, but a little later, herself washed, gargled and rinsed, she absent-mindedly slips them on again and faces the world through familiar flecks and speckles. She prepares lunch for herself and my dad, who has been up for hours, and after he has served the coffee and she has cleared away the debris, my mother unfolds her sewing once again. I don't know how she manages to thread her needle. Her deep set, caramel eyes squint patiently through the foggy spectacles as she holds up her plump arms. But her stubby, dimpled fingers seem to have developed eyes of their own. My mother is eighty years old. She has been threading needles for three-quarters of a century. Her hands have, in fact, become the instruments of her vision.

What are you doing, mama?
> *Oh, I'm making something.*
> *What's it going to be?*
> *We'll see. Maybe it'll work into a doll.*
> *Who's it for?*
> *A child, somewhere.*

Why do you make dolls, mama?
> *To please the children.*
> *Only the children?*
> *Who else?*
> *I like your dolls.*
> *So?*
> *I'm a middle-aged woman.*
> *You're still my child.*

How often, over the years, have I rephrased those questions, trying to find the words to pierce her apparent innocence.

But mama, what are you really doing when you make your dolls? What does it mean to you?
> *I don't like to sit with empty hands. So I think, 'Maybe I'll give a child some pleasure.'*
> *What about the button pictures then, and all the other things you make up out of your head?*
> *When I get tired of making dolls, I think, 'Maybe I'll try something else for a change.'*

I remain dissatisfied. The dolls themselves clamour that there is more to it; so much more, proclaim those bright and dancing pictures. What does she know? Doesn't she know how much she knows?

Certainly, when I first set out to trace the creative process in this apparently simple manifestation, my innocently productive mother, I didn't know how much I didn't know. How much less then, could I gauge the degree of her comprehension, or, for that matter, the degree of validity of my assumption that everything she knew had to be translatable into the language of words? Why should she have to explain her dolls to me? I get irritated when people ask me to explain my books. The work is its own explanation. And yet, because I think that human creativity is so vital to human well-being, and so little understood, and so undervalued in our society, in spite of all the brouhaha to the contrary, I feel that it may be of use for me to try to reproduce, as accurately as I can, what she has helped me to learn. Who would have thought, nearly thirty years ago, when I set out in the full presumption of my college education, to be an ARTIST, that the years of search would bring me, in middle age, to kneel as a small child again, at my mother's needles?

She certainly has no aspiration to create ART. Her aesthetic values haven't all been neatly cleaned and pressed to fit cultural top drawers. She sometimes asks me, genuinely puzzled, why I talk so much about the dolls and the pictures and the junk creations, and hardly ever mention her beautiful cutwork tablecloths. The first time I brought my collection of her work to give a talk and doll show at the University of Manitoba, she was really worried about what would happen to me. She didn't want me to make a fool of myself and come away hurt. She didn't want people to laugh at me. Why would educated people want to hear about her dolls?

I will not try to evaluate her works here as art objects. Like all truly unique, created things, they make their own moment. I am not here to measure and weigh. I am here to discover and enjoy, to reveal and share. I am here to trace and celebrate the most generous impulse, and the most mysterious process known to man, the impulse to create, the process of creation. If I can illuminate, however faintly, the work in the spirit of its making, I will gladly leave the weighing and measuring, the evaluating and pigeonholing to others.

The human creator brings into being something which is in some way different from what has been brought to public consciousness before. Although his means are often profoundly subjective, his end result is transcendently objective. He produces a self-consistent, coherent whole which can function totally separately from himself. In whatever métier, the creator goes where none he knows has been before, and maps the course. Thereafter, the world is enlarged for those who can read his language.

By language I mean, of course, the means by which he seizes and objectifies his perceptions, the symbol system through which he creates and communicates what he knows. There are any number of languages, any number of symbol systems which represent different ways of probing reality, different ways of knowing. Poetry, music, painting, sculpture, mathematics are but a few. Sometimes a creative spirit will master a craft to the point where he or she can begin to expand its potentiality as a language; she makes of it an art form through which she enlarges our perceptions, our comprehension, our world. Great potters are such. My mother is one such, too, I believe. And because the métier of the seamstress is not an intimidating one, I hope to be able to use her and her work as the basis for my discussion of creativity, and to use this discussion as an excuse to share my pleasure in her work. I stress the non-threatening nature of her activity because whenever one tries to approach the subject of creativity through those manifestations to which most lip-service is paid in our society, capitalized ART or SCIENCE, people feel impelled to don masks, take up attitudes, strike poses, affirm stances, mount hobby horses, go all heady and rarefied, or simply retreat altogether, which latter is the humble expedient of people who consider themselves simple, ordinary folk, and have been trained on that account not to expect much of themselves when confronted with capitalized prestige.

These attitudes are ingrained very early. All my childhood I heard about how only ten people in the world could understand Einstein, if that many. Not having any pronounced mathematical bent, and never having come near seeing the point of the grade ten physics I never mastered, I despaired of ever comprehending concepts in which I was, in fact, acutely interested. Similarly, in my day it was the going word among North Winnipeg grade school children (and how many children since) that when you reached a certain grade, you were condemned to try to read that grimace, ugh, *SHAKESPEARE*. Yah! I happened to be lucky. When I repeated this information to my big sister she sat me down on the bed and read to me from one of the Comedies. The laughter of that afternoon rescued a whole, for me supremely relevant, universe.

Interestingly enough, through much exploration and examination and interpretation and weighing and measuring and familiarization and controversy, the universe of Einstein is no longer so utterly incomprehensible. Increasingly familiar with the idea of its existence, we have proceeded to colonize it. We have even watched new worlds being charted beyond. And even those of us who cannot repeat with much comprehension the magic equation have some grasp of its implications. Created worlds can be rejected, they can be misinterpreted, they can be distorted, they can be ignored, they can be colonized, they can be lost, they can be rediscovered, they can be superseded, they can be reinterpreted, they can be passed on, they can even be comprehended, and they can be destroyed. They exist in the same flux as the rest of us, created beings all.

No one is likely to consider my mother's language abstruse and incomprehensible, or to respond by going uptight and high-falutin, or alternately all humble before this spectacle of a little old woman at play. Her output functions outside our society's preferred structure of REAL VALUES, nor does it threaten TO LAST, so there is no need to strike attitudes before it. The effect is disarming; people respond directly, with a curiously ingenuous innocence which is rather touching to see. Often the reaction is quite strong. "Let's get out of here, they're driving me nuts," I heard one young woman say urgently to her companion, at one of my doll shows. Of course, if you encounter a genuinely other world, which seems to be communicating at some disturbing level with your own, you must expect to be dislocated even while you are being relocated. If it is the work of an artist, you may be expected to assimilate disturbing and intense emotions, to adjust to an apparently untranslatable coherence. What would it have been like to disembark from a Western vessel on the shores of Japan, a century or so ago?

Often, it is the negative emotional reaction to a new creation which tells most surely that something real is happening. Since we spend much of our lives battening down our vulnerabilities, barricading our weak spots, putting up a tangle of defences against even the thought of pain and discomfort, and since every established mode develops accretions of vested interest, the demand that is made by the newly created, whether it be art or idea, that we open up to an unknown, is often fanatically resisted. We fear it the more vehemently because in fact it is not completely unknown. It exists as potential under our battened hatches, in our padlocked closets, in our crouching souls. Recoil and non-comprehension are defences of fear against growth, which, like any change, we tend to perceive as a kind of death. For growth invariably involves disturbances, the accommodation of feelings sometimes painful, and the threat to current equilibrium. Self-conscious artists proceed in the full knowledge that this is likely to be the effect of their work. They are aware of its strangeness. Fiction writers, while pursuing and surrendering to the logic of their imaginings, are often afraid that they must be going out of their minds. I've had this fear expressed to me with great conviction by fellow novelists in the throes, and have felt it myself, acutely. But I've never known it to discourage an artist. If anything, it's a spur, like the thought of having a terminal heart attack during sex, preferably at ninety. What a way to die! Somehow you know you're on to something, and if it's to be madness, it's madness in a good cause. For self-conscious artists are usually convinced that what they are doing is important, and will somehow help to reconcile us to our own skeletons, that we may better assume the human shape.

It would distress my mother, however, to think that her work is capable of disturbing anyone's equilibrium. She doesn't realize that she is essentially, to the extent that she is a creator, a maverick; she can't help asserting the validity of her own reality, launching her assertions into concrete, independent being. And here they are, defined, separate, existing as insistently in their own medium as any Adam, when God cut the thread.

As I hope to show, there are other significant characteristics which she shares with more sophisticated creators. But even her apparent differences from them can be revealing. She is certainly free of the more worldly aspects of artistic aspiration. She has "vaulting ambition" for neither fame, money, nor permanence. Her very medium is fragile and impermanent. This is not to say that she creates disposable art; such an idea would be offensive to her because she abhors waste, as an indignity to the wasted. However, the idea of permanence for her dolls, or herself, their persistence for some unspecified "ever," would be merely puzzling to her, as contradicting what she knows to be true, that it's not nature's way.

You mean to say you made this one for a child? Look how delicate it is. A kid would rip it apart in two minutes.
> *So, I'll fix it.*
> *There'll be nothing left to fix.*

> So I'll make another.
> But mama . . .

How to put it so as to get her to say something—what is it I want to hear? As a child, I remember, for many years I had this nagging feeling that there was something there but missing, something I wasn't being told, couldn't quite comprehend. I remember being very patient about it, very obedient about not discussing certain recurring topics labelled "private" with anybody, trusting that when the time came surely my parents would enlighten me. As usually happens, a schoolmate got there first with hotted-up verbal enlightenment. I can still remember sitting in the lush green park, stunned and throbbing, having suddenly had THE FACTS OF LIFE revealed to me in pithy vernacular. I look at mama's dolls and I know there is still something she hasn't told me yet.

— Why do you make dolls, mama? —

Certainly not for money. She has never sold a doll. She meets the occasional suggestion that she could make money by selling her dolls, with quelling disdain:

> *Sell my dolls? All my life I worked alongside my husband, to earn a piece of bread, to help bring up my children, to educate them. Now I don't need to sell my hands.*

I can't even guess how many dolls she has made over the past quarter century, though I suspect well over a thousand, not to mention embroidery and button and junk pictures, and appliqué and fur wall hangings, and other creations. Dolls for grandchildren, for sick children, for neighbouring children, friends' children, relatives' children, unknown children, grown-up children, any and all children, all given freely, as though making and giving are the most natural acts a liberated spirit can achieve. Her basic impulse is to share, to communicate, to contribute, and I think this is characteristic. Even where there are no known audiences, no expected rewards, the act of creation is essentially a generous, social gesture. Of course it is legitimate for creative people to yearn also for recognition and reward. Payment is, if nothing more, brute survival currency. And creators, the celebrators of life and its potential, like, no less than anyone else, to be able to live well. One of the most fascinating and pathetic documents I have ever read was a volume of Mozart's letters. Poverty, debt, family and personal ill health, desperate casting about for financial help, all these were the constant biographical accompaniment to his composition and performance. And throughout that short lifetime of bone-jarring journeys from one noble establishment to another, there runs as repeated refrain the somewhat wistful prayer that this time the relevant nobleman will pay him in money, instead of grandly bestowing upon him a handsome watch on his departure. Mozart went on composing anyway, but a better-used Mozart might have survived beyond thirty-six years, to compose a little longer. We are as cavalier about our human as about our other resources, and the loss is, ultimately, our own.

It is rare indeed that the pure creative impulse survives a lifetime, to come into its own, finally, and function in its own ideal terms. That is why I continued to question my mother, in what must have seemed to her a tediously repetitive way. But to me, cracking mom's code took on a quest-like urgency, as time passed. Innocently productive, artistically naive, if she could be brought to articulate the why of herself and her work, not only might we come to understand better the kind of being she is, but we might learn something about the phenomenon of creativity itself, so that we might begin to deal more intelligently with the children, among whom so few survive to be seminally productive, lone guerrillas the world over, in school systems and societies which would destroy them, though professing always the best of intentions.

I am not trying to say that we would all become Einsteins or Mozarts. I repeat, I am not here to measure and weigh, and compare endowments. Enough, surely, that if not we, our children might someday be encouraged to grow into a fuller, more satisfying humanity, instead of being pared and trimmed to the unfulfilled, incomplete adulthood of which I have heard so many complain. The dead-end cries, "Is this all there is to life?" and "Is this all that life has to offer me?," while they express real malaise, express also a passive, consumer's orientation to existence. Life is limited to what you're alive to. If you want more you must commit yourself to making more. Life is expansible. Creativity is a natural human attribute, which we all share, to some degree, and of which too few of us ever get to know the pleasure, in ourselves or in others like us. Why?

———————————

Educators tell us that most children are spontaneously creative. What happens? It is not my purpose here to embark on a critique of education systems. The inherent dilemma educators face seems obvious: how to teach what must be taught for the perpetuation of a civilization, without cutting off the child's potential for contributing creatively to the continuous renewal and transformation of that civilization? Teachers can teach only what they know. But the creative urge teases us toward what we don't quite know yet, toward different ways of knowing. The motivated, creative child often finds himself at loggerheads with the formal educative process, and lonely in the world he is drawn to explore. And yet he is lucky, if not always happy, for in a profound sense he has been put in touch with himself, and will fight overtly or secretly, consciously or blindly, to protect what he senses to be crucial. One of my mother's grandchildren has been involved, practically since babyhood, in the advanced study of sub-atomic physics. As a little kid he read formulae the way I read literature now. I asked J.J. once, when he was thirteen, how the physics was coming.

Well, you know auntie, I don't get much time in the morning. I have to take the dog for a walk and get ready for school. And then it's a long bus ride to school and back. And when I get home I have my chores to do, and my homework. I'm pretty tired by night-time. So I save all my thinking for the weekends.

What of the many children who don't yet know what unique paths they might explore? The child for whom every act still has alternatives, who is still, that is, spontaneously creative in possibility, learns very early, through pressure from adult and peer, that not only the destructively anti-social, but all maverick impulses, are not worth pursuing. As part of the very process by which we civilize and educate him, society also sets about pruning the bright, joyous shoots of what it sees as wayward growth. I once heard Buckminster Fuller describe it in a radio interview as "pinching off." There is a whole area of my own psyche that is still black and blue in testimony to the pinches I survived, and I am sure the ghost of that sloppy, angry, disconsolate little girl still hangs about those cloakrooms and corridors and principals' offices to which I was so frequently banished. Other children expend much of their spirit in simply learning to live with their mutilations, and preparing to spend their lives squeezed between those neat margins my teachers were so fanatical about.

For each sacrifice of potential self, we console the child by dangling before him the carrot of the future. "Someday" he will no longer be vulnerable; he will be grown up and everything will be possible, all of life will be open to him. To smooth his path toward the spurious apotheosis of adulthood, he gives up real independence of thought and feeling at the time when his responses are still at their most flexible. He learns that what is important is not how to think but what to think, not how to cope with his feelings but what to feel about, not how to be responsive but what to respond to. Growing up becomes a process of discarding, at each stage, the felt sense of our various ages, our own former selves.

You're not a baby any more!
Stop being so childish!
How adolescent!
Aren't you a bit past that?

How hostile we are urged to become to our own selves in passing. Worst of all, we eventually manage to persuade the child to discard, as a disdained vestige of babyhood, a part of what every human being should retain as his inherent gift throughout his life, the desire and ability, in some area at least, to continue to question playfully, to play seriously, to discover and remake some small portion of his world anew, and to respond to the newness of another's making. For of course the other vital end of the creative act is the ability of the receiver of the gift to respond.

One of the characteristics I have noticed in creative people is that they retain about them something still alive of all the ages through which they have passed. It's as though when pressed by society to turn in the attributes of childhood in exchange for those of adolescence, they have secretly held some childhood back, clinging to the continuing sense of the validity of that childhood space, and so too when the time is decreed for the turning in of adolescence in exchange for all the formal gear of adulthood. They have somehow refused to pass through their lives as tourists. Harrowed they may be, plagued by apparently irreconcilable elements, labelled neurotics, branded as irresponsible, and even anti-social, they have nevertheless retained a sense of the reality, not merely the memory, of the ages through which they have lived. Of course, on the negative side, they often retain also the shortcomings, the "immaturities" of the ages they have refused to relinquish. Childlike, yes, and sometimes childish too, these creators. They have more of the entire stretch of their felt-lifespace to range in than is normally approved, a lifespace which, since one is never quite what one used to be, necessarily partakes of all the dangers and excitements and anxieties of paradox, of co-existing multiple dimension, of binary simultaneity, of flux in search of form, of things to be made in search of their maker. We have heard a great deal in the past few years of the expanding of consciousness, mainly in connection with artificial means of in fact dislocating consciousness. It is my conviction that the kind of enlargement of consciousness to which I refer and will refer again is far more relevant to human achievement.

Even in our era of encapsulated age groupings, my mother retains recognizably something of the magic and sadness and vulnerability and joy of every age she has known. She's what the kids used to call "with it." A free citizen of the spirit, she is a margin-hopper, a tester, a rearranger and transformer of the boundaries to which most of us cling blindly as we feel our way through life. People of all ages respond to her, reach out to her, confide in her, perceive her not as a trespasser, for she does not presume on their literal actuality, but as an ageless peer. I have heard a number of times, often from people I scarcely know, that she is considered a "wise woman." Perhaps. She is also an innocent and incorrigible force of nature, who, under the impression that she is decorating life's margins, opens up new worlds beyond.

Her dolls, however decorative, are not mere bland fantasies. I am always astonished by the range and variety of recognizable expression, of character interpretation, of mood and individuality of response. See, for example, this simplest of all group of five small, rag and puppet dolls. Their heads are made of cut-out bits of foam rubber. The faces have been created by a combination of incision and stitching. The biggest head is perhaps an inch and a half in diameter. And yet each one has a distinct and striking way of facially addressing herself to the world. Each is unique, in structure and expression. There is no doubt that each of these rag and foam little ladies is a character. One or two may even be character assassins. I call the group my coffee klatch, for obvious reasons.

Sometimes I will look from doll to doll, concentrating on the button eyes through which so many of them gaze. Who would have imagined that button eyes could be made so variously expressive?

Aha, I think at first, it's the way she's got that stitch, or those two stitches, or three, which sew the button to the face, and provide the pupil. It's the colour and slant of the stitch. But it's also the shape and size of the button, and its relation to the nose, and the shape of the nose, and its size and position in relation to the eyes. The material counts too, the complexion, its colour and texture. And the mouth, yes, the kind of stitch and colour of thread and particular curve of the mouth, its distance from the nose, how it relates to the eyes. And the shape of the face and the bulge of the cheek, the chin, the forehead, hair, that ridiculous hat! Those eyebrows, too! AND the costume, the costume! That use of colour, that sense of design . . .

And I am drawn, in spite of myself, once again into the particular coherence of that particular doll, to the recognition of a unique organization, the subtle playing off of contradictions and harmonies which produces a new harmony-in-contradiction, a new fitness, a new particular unity, a new person clamouring his authenticity, her reality.

For a while, for want of space, I had many of the dolls pinned up all over the bookcase in the room where I was working. The dark mottle of bookspines did not provide the best of backgrounds to show them off clearly; nevertheless the juxtaposition was peculiarly fitting. Those dolls could have come from those books. They are a version in another form of what those books are all about, life.

Can all this be accident? Am I reading into the dolls more than is there? Are the combinations and results which I perceive fortuitous, chance arrangements? Accident clearly has its place here, as in any complex organization; chance, or accident, is an important element, a gift, *donné*, which the creator is quick to seize. But the important thing is the mind which is willing to see the accident as incident, to perceive relevance through it, to solicit accident with all humility, and then to harness it in the service of revelation.

In eighty years Chaika Waisman has seen many changes. During most of that time she has been a dressmaker, involved in a craft which not only reflects changes, but in the Western world demands them, creates them, and measures its own vitality and health by its ability to remain in constant flux, and tease human vanity along with it. Change is the oxygen in the stream of fashion. And for those who like to remain in midstream it's a constant and giddy rush, as I learned when I complimented a young cousin on a pair of slacks she was wearing and she replied, "Yes, but they're four months out of style."

At eighty, mama still knows what "they're wearing" this

season. At the same time she ranges freely among the fashions of her lifetime, combining and redesigning. She responds not only to the styles, but to the underlying states of mind which they suggest and reflect. She is, for instance, stimulated by the eclectic dress of what she calls the "nowadays children." Some of the dolls are entertaining comments, from a very mod old lady, on sexual and social attitudes of our time. She examines liberated fashion with as much gusto and indifference to the fixed claims of the traditions which one would expect her to represent, as any media and peer-infatuated youngster convinced that he is in the forefront of a daring rebellion. At the same time, within all the flux and confusion of change, she points up what nevertheless remains stable, relevant, and unchanging, and it is the juxtaposition of the two apparently incongruous realities in one little fabricated creature which so often brings out, in the startled viewer, an involuntary exclamation of laughter.

See, I've brought you a nowadays couple.

What could be more mod than these elongated forms? What could better evoke the spirit of glittering tattiness of our youth than these two nylon stockings stuffed with bits and pieces of coloured cloth? Only suggestively humanoid, they are nevertheless no less so than those cadaverous models of the fashion magazines in which the wills of the designers seek to direct or define the whims of the public.

> *This is the boy,* she explains, stroking the long, blond, silk drape-cord hair. *You know how the boys wear their hair nowadays, and with a fancy band.*
> > *And this one is the girl?* I examine the dog-eared doll carefully. *How can you tell?*
> Mama is surprised. *Can't you see she's pregnant?*

Sure enough, the essential falls into place, rebuking my faulty perceptions.

She's carrying high, mother murmurs.

I am particularly fond of these dolls, because they illustrate for me a phenomenon highly prized by creatively active people. Sometimes, in psychology textbooks, we come across a picture, usually a geometrical figure-ground design, which illustrates a phenomenon known, I think, by some such name as visual perception shift. We are told to stare at the illustration concentratedly, until we experience a visual shift, in which the figure-ground relationship of the picture is suddenly reversed. Background becomes foreground; foreground has receded; another pattern dominates. At a more complex level, in the area of ideas, similar shifts are key events. For many years we had saved our nylon stockings to send to mom so she could stuff her dolls. Obviously there came a point when she looked at a nylon stocking and was inspired, experiencing, through a leap of the imagination, the revelation of the nylon stocking. Instead of the guts of the doll the stocking was now perceived as the potential skin, and a new era of dollhood emerged, during which, in a whole spate of little creatures, she explored the implications of this initial transformation of idea, and worked out numerous corollary problems and solutions. The shape of the stockings, for instance, dictated the elongated form of the dolls, just as in the heel could be perceived the possibility of pregnancy. Their transparency and flexibility suggested the colourful stuffing of gaily cut-up bits of soft cloth. All of this subtly dictated the character of the dolls, their individual "styles."

In the ensuing years she has tried many different kinds of stuffings for a whole variety of "skins," and experimented with all kinds of aesthetic effects related to variations of the form and type of the basic initial innovation. I have coarse-skinned nylon onion bags bristly with vivid, lumpy chunks of sturdy cloth, the very character of the dolls, their large noses and bold features and the freeform

caricatural gestures of their shapes determined by the coarser nature of sack and suited materials sticking out of the larger skin holes. Out of soft, large mesh-coloured stockings loosely filled with coloured rags I have a big, floppy octopus, with two flash bulbs for eyes and a barbell-shaped rattle for a flourish at the top of its variegated head. This perception of the possibility of other kinds of "skin," I suspect, freed her to go on to experiment with a whole series of bottle dolls, filling some transparent bottles with colourful scraps of paper and cloth, and "dressing" other plastic jugs in such a way that their basic shapes suggest and provide the dolls with some of their individual character. The jugs with handles, for instance, often become elegant, one-bare-shoulder-and-armed-ladies. I suspect that the form of the jug urges itself on the open imagination, much as a teapot has somehow that magical, abstractly humanoid shape, as well as suggestiveness of function, which is reputed, traditionally, to be so popular in the transformation fantasies of the insane. Size, shape, texture of skins determine the kinds of stuffings, textures, colours, and type of limbs and features, the general "character" of the doll which eventually emerges. Form and content determine each other in that always subtle unity in interaction which will puzzle critics forever.

So the artist, in her trance of concentration, in the intensity of her inner focus, courts vision and revelation, sees new possibilities, explores new forms within form, wrestles with all the changing possible forms of form, and relationships of idea to particular form, and fixes each captured shape for our astonishment while she continues to engage the ever-changing mystery. I have seen this process of inspiration express itself in mother's work numberless times over the years, and each time have watched a rich vein of possibility work itself out with impeccable logic in a flood of dolls and other creations. It's a bit like watching a whole school of art working out all the implications of the breakthrough premises of its founders, or like seeing a Picasso work single-handedly through them all. What amazes me is that there seems to be no end to her possible flow, for she responds with utter freedom and flexibility to the potential in all she sees, combining and recombining in ways ever unexpected, ever new.

I first noticed that mother was using bits of fish skeleton in her work when she brought me a doll with the beautiful vertebrae of the "Coony," as it's called in Winnipeg, for eyes. "Coony" is a vulgarization of "L'Inconnu," the name given by French explorers to a fish they were at first unable to identify. Nowadays it's been tagged as a distant relative of the whitefish. Smoked, rich and meaty, the Coony is a very popular item of North Winnipeg delicatessen. Mom saves the vertebrae, scrubs them, dries them, and uses them in pictures, on dolls, and, alternating them with dried pumpkin, watermelon, orange, lemon and grapefruit seeds, and any other items that lend themselves to her purpose, including wishbones and the cleaned and dried bones of chicken and turkey necks, she makes necklaces of them. I noticed a curiously attractive little ornament on her coat one day, and on closer inspection discovered a cluster of frog's leg bones set off by red embroidery thread, testimony to an ever-expanding culinary and aesthetic horizon.

One day my sister, keeping mom busy during a visit, bought a whole variety of fish for her to make gefilte fish. To mom's delight, the basic carp had not yet been dressed and trimmed. "You don't often get a whole carp with his tail still on in the shops nowadays." She thereupon abstracted the carp's magnificent tail, cleaned, "cured" and dried it, and proceeded to make me a "mermaid," the first of a whole spate of sea creatures, hangings, pictures and ornaments. I don't often name the dolls, but Circé Dugong seemed to name herself. By some intuitive process, mother, who had, in Florida, seen the sea cows of the type who are said to have inspired the mermaid fantasies in sea-bushed sailors, though I don't know whether she knew of the connection, somehow managed to com-

bine the superb, blowsy ugliness of the dugong, or manatee, with the seductive, soft shape and texture, the womanly suggestiveness of a Circé. Maybe it's something in those buggy-out huge costume jewellery pearl eyes, or that rakish little tam in the same mottled green-black velvety textured material as the body, or the cushiony seal-like shape of the body itself. It could be the cloth strips of flowing blonde hair, or the barbie-type doll shoe nose. Whatever, Circé is for me the ultimate mermaid, comic integration of myth and reality.

Mom's independence, her resistance to received notions is exemplified in Circé's "man." She has been told a number of times by people anxious to instruct her in correct mythology, that the appropriate partner for a mermaid is a sailor. Nevertheless she insists that the clown she made for the mating purpose suits our Circé D. just fine. Why should she do what everybody else does? she queries. What people don't immediately seem to notice is the curious intuitive note, the fact that though the clown is clearly no sailor, his eyes are two sides of a miniature toy London double-decker bus. Circé's man has had travel in his eyes all along.

If you get close enough to Circé D., you can smell her fishtail. You would therefore be able to identify her, to use the impressive language of art scholarship, as Clara Waisman, Early Fishbone Period. Late Fishbone is the period after the artist had wrestled with and overcome a problem of practical craft of the kind which original minds must frequently confront. My mother, during the early period of fascination with the fish as craft material, made several dolls and hangings for my nephew, in warmly damp and aromatic Miami. They proved irresistible to his cats, who managed to eat all the bones and fishtails off all the pictures and dolls. So she set herself to invent a cleansing and curing process which would solve the problem of lingering odours. And this she did. In Middle Waisman Fishbone the aroma is faint. In Late Waisman Fishbone I can't smell a thing.

One of the joys of any kind of creative activity is in its stimulation of the human delight in problem-solving. The pleasure in overcoming obstacles encourages further engagement, and the creator is drawn ever more deeply into possibility. But of course purpose and particular function will determine the limits of particular kinds of experimentation. At the simplest level, for instance, mom would never put a button or anything potentially harmful on a doll intended for a small baby's use. These are always soft and plump and cuddly and harmless. Considerations of form and function, social choice, as well as the perception of relevance limit creative possibilities at any given time or place. Perhaps that is why so frequently in past ages men have actually made discoveries which have been ignored, or just-missed making discoveries which we celebrate pridefully having made in recent ages. Though it's been there, potentially, all along, we only gradually begin to see what is becoming relevant within the social context. Once an idea, a world view, a new organization, a new rhythm becomes significant, or potentially useful to the evolving pattern of a society, it is not only likely to be discovered, but is occasionally even discovered simultaneously by more than one mind sensitized in the appropriate direction. This is true not only in the sciences.

One day, several years ago, while riding along the 401 en route from Montreal to Toronto, I noticed two signs on one post, which together read ODESSA— YARKER. "Odessa-Yarker," I remarked to my husband. "Say, wouldn't that be a great name for a character?" And sure enough, within the next three years or so Odessa Yarker did become a character in a play, a character of whom I am particularly fond, as she echoes and resounds at so many levels for me, not the least of which, somehow, is the joke of her beginning. A very personal, idiosyncratic, private bit of discovery-creation, wouldn't you say? I had completed the great, as yet undiscovered play in which Odessa Yarker is prominently featured, and having settled near Toronto, we were sitting and chatting with a new friend, a fellow writer, the gifted novelist Marian Engel. "I've just finished writing a children's book," Marian remarked cheerfully. "You'll never guess what it's called. I call it MY NAME IS NOT ODESSA YARKER." Marian had never heard of my play or my character. Who had? But that sign, that juxtaposition had been waiting for the right time, the right kind of sensibility, the right climate of awareness, at which point the names of two small towns in Ontario took on instantaneous life and hitchhiked like extra-terrestrial visitors in a science fiction story, into the minds of two separate Canadian writers, there to germinate separately and be separately born.

That this is a phenomenon not easily grasped by many academic minds has been made clear to me in requests I get from thesis-writing students, one of whom sent me recently the names of two books whose characters and situations were suspected of having influenced my novels. She apologized for this, saying that her pro-fessors wanted her to trace a "tradition." As it happens, one of the books I'd never read; the other I read, and enjoyed, just recently, years after having written my own novel. This linear literal-mindedness reveals a lack of understanding of the part cultural climate plays in coaxing imaginative minds independently to simi-lar constructions.

It is obvious by now that though I am writing primarily about creativity, the creative impulse and the creative process as I have perceived them in my mother, her life and her work, I shall not hesitate, where necessary, to use my own experience as a writer, a child, a mother, a teacher, or in whatever capacity, to clarify or supplement my observations. And though I shall be putting forward any number of arguments, and making any number of assertions, with which you may or may not agree, my main object is to re-create the reality from which the arguments spring, for argu-ments are judgments of and abstractions from the felt quality of experience, and give a pitiably thinned-out version of what one knows. I can assess far better the quality of what a person knows if I am given to understand how he or she knows it, and even more if I can recreate his or her experience of it. And though the created thing can be approached as a separate, objective fact, the process of its making will never be apprehended in the coarse nets of strictly linear thought.

As one who has spent much of her life searching, oh so seriously, to find a small niche within at least occasional viewing distance, on a clear day, of that "great good place" where, as Henry James has suggested, all true creators would like to dwell, it is surely understandable that I should be intrigued by the fact that every time visibility has been blessedly good enough for me to catch a glimpse of that harmonious inner courtyard wherein bubbles eternally the magic source, my mother has been sitting there, contentedly at home, playing in the fountain at the heart of creation.

Where does it begin?

I must be very young; my mother is still singing, all the time. I am the third of four living children, but at this moment we are alone. I play beside her on the couch while she dusts the sunroom windowsills. There are five round-arched windows. The woodwork is tawny, red gold. When my mother sings the neighbour comes out of his house and into our yard and stretches himself out on our lawn. I gaze at her fine, pink face, glowing in the window light. Her dark hair has small, tight tight tight waves. They glow in the light. Everything glows. I am aglow with the rapture of the revelation that she is the most beautiful in the whole world, my mother. I am too young to ask, 'Why me? How come I am chosen?' I belong to what is given. It is an intensely aesthetic pleasure, experienced, thank goodness, before the pinched and crabbed world with its penny-ruler measurements interposed its decrees that her nose is too long, her eyes too deeply set, baffling the child's

intuitive perceptions, my unerring love. Thank you, formal
education, thank you, herd standards, but no thank you, too.
Long is the unlearning of your learning, glad the return to
vision.

EXPERIENTIAL CONCLUSIONS:

FROM THE BEGINNING, AND SOMETIMES EVEN WITH THE
BEST OF INTENTIONS, SOCIETY CONSPIRES TO ROB THE
CHILD OF HIS OWN EXPERIENCE.

CHILDREN WHO LEARN TOO WELL ARE THOSE MOST CHEATED
BY THEIR EDUCATION.

PERSISTENTLY CREATIVE CHILDREN RETAIN WIDE, SLOPPY
MARGINS FOR UNLEARNING, O'ERLEAPING AND TRANSFORM-
ING.

UNLESSON:

Who has not heard of the hands of the artist? Long, slim,
sensitive hands, of course. As a youngster I thought, "Well, that
lets us out." The Wisemans have what, as far as I could gather,
were to be universally deplored as "pudgy hands." And yet,
the most helpless hands I've subsequently known were long,
slim, sensitive and artistic-looking, and at their best when kept
in the lap where they could be admired and not get in the way
when it came to doing things. Conversely, once, aboard ship, I
watched, unnoticed, an ugly, runty, hairy, bow-legged little
skew-eyed mate absorbed in painting an ancient dory in
anticipation of a day's fishing. There was not an unlovely line
or movement in that entire afternoon's labour. For there is
nothing like the grace of whatever shape of hand or body in
the sureness of making.

My mother's hands are chubby and small, her fingertips are

needle-toughened and sometimes painfully cracked. But they sew on with unselfconscious skill. And from them a world emerges, my mother's world. For if you're lucky, as I think my mother has been lucky, at some time during the indenture of your lifetime, nature may grant you the freedom, within your limited means, to transform your means, the freedom to create.

What is freedom?

> The Chinese calligrapher, they say, seeking perfection, was enslaved to his stroke, which he practised, day after day, year after year, all his life long. And then one day he found that his stroke had become his wing.

> *Mama, why do you and daddy sew all the time?*
> > *So you won't have to. You won't be a dressmaker.*
> > *You're not kidding.*
> > *Mind you, my child, ten skilled fingers will always keep you alive. But if you rely on them, and know no other cunning, then you must keep them going day and night if you want to educate your children to an easier life.*

Well I learned to understand the economics of ten fingers. I could see and smell and hear how that worked, every stitch of the way, the rattle of the sewing machines, the rasping snap of the big scissors, the sizzle of the steaming cloth, the rank-smelling steam from old clothes, impregnated with sweat, the thud of the heavy wooden steaming block, the curve of my parents' bodies as they handstitched for hours, those terrible, lengthy sessions with the customers as they fitted and refitted. Oh the customers! How they niggled and naggled, how they wheedled and bullied and haggled, how they changed and rechanged and changed again their minds, while my parents stitched and pulled stitches and stitched again. And we children, listening behind the curtain to the traffic of grown-up life, sensed the pressure of cramped and frustrated lives behind the pettiness of human beings, and recoiled. Oh yes, I understood well enough why we were, all four of us, to be hoisted on those bent shoulders to a better life.

For my father the needle was a weapon, inadequate, but to be plied nevertheless with scrupulous competence, minuscule sword that stitched on and on, winning each day's survival, piling up a lifetime of small but crucial victories. When they first came to Canada, he worked a ninety-six hour week in the factories, determined to conquer the new world for his children. Thrown out of work during the depression, he moved his family out of my mother's little dream house with the arched windows and the fringed silk windowblinds, rented out the house, and moved in behind a shopfront, his plans unchanged. If it was not to be a fulfilment of his pre-orphan dreams of cantorial glory and rabbinical scholarship for himself, it was at least an honourable standoff that he would claim from life, while his children studied. But his underlying dislike of the whole business made it necessary for mom to be doubly alert. He especially hated lengthy fittings, and when the customer was giving him a hard time, he would become increasingly impatient. Very often he was completely justified in his annoyance. But we could not afford to lose the pennies. So mom would hastily leave her chores, slip through the curtain which separated our living quarters from the shop, and somehow manage to soothe and placate. Even she, I'm happy to say, lost patience sometimes, and I remember one or two epic moments when she finally drew her four feet some inches up to her full seven feet, and announced to a customer, "I'm sorry, we can no longer deal with you."

How we kids cheered, silently, when that happened. If the result was a tightening of belts it was not our belts that were to show it. We could hear them up front as we ate, for the plasterboard walls reached only about three-quarters of the way to the ceiling of our makeshift honeycomb, those years when we lived behind the storefront. We would go to sleep with the sound of the streetcars roaring up and turning into the old North Main car barns across the street, and the closer spurting whir of the sewing machines from up front. And when we awoke, occasionally, into the never-quite darkness the streetlamps provided, we knew it must be very late because the streetcars were silent, though not the sewing machines. Sometimes, on our way out to school we would find our parents in the shop, dad sitting asleep on folded arms at the sewing machine, and mom curled up on the cutting table, too tired, when finally unable to stitch any longer, to find their way back to their couch in the kitchen.

Mama, why did you become a dressmaker? You didn't have to. You said your daddy didn't even want you to.
> *Because I loved it.*

Baffling replies. How could you love what enslaved you? And how could she, through all of this, continue to tell us kids that "Work will make your life sweet!" How I used to hoot and snort and threaten to puke over that one.

And yet, she loved us too, no small enslavement. She was an anxious mother, and no wonder.

At eleven months their first child developed an inflammation of the lungs. The only help available was the local Felscher, a partially trained medical assistant. Itzhok was dying. My mother heard that the great Ukrainian doctor of the district was attending a wealthy neighbour. She ran. She pleaded to see him though she knew he did not like Jews. She actually knelt before him, begging him to save her child.
> *There are more important people to save than your son.*

And when they were stealing their way across the Russian border en route to Canada, in the middle of the night, they came to a river. One of the peasant guides took their new hope, the six-week-old Marjm. As they stepped into the water, the man carrying my sister whispered, "If the child cries I'll drown her."

How often, in my childhood, I heard the passionately uttered words, "We must bring our children to a shore!"

How long have you been sewing, mama?
> *Oh, I was still a child, three, four, maybe five. Next door we had a little dressmaker, not what you would call a real modiste. She wasn't trained, but she tried, by herself, to do simple work. She used to gather together rags, and whenever she saw me she gave them to me, and I started to work out all kinds of toys and dolls and doll clothes and flowers. I took to those. It meant to me . . . the whole world.*
> *You didn't make them when we were kids.*
> *Who had time?*

Housework, sewing, customers: how, when you have your work always in your hands, do you keep four children from straying? When we lived in the house on Burrows Ave., we were the only kids on the block who had a swing and sandbox in our backyard. But mainly, in those days, my mother held us near her with words. She kept us on the long leash of an endless rope of language, looping and knotting us as firmly to her as ever she stitched edge to edge in a seam. She lassoed us daily and webbed us and gilded our lives with innumerable threads of prose. Words spun about us; sometimes the very air was afog with words that purled like a fine mist about our ears: stories and persuasions and fantasies and cajolings and adjurations and just plain fast-talking that fogged up your brain with ideas, intoxicated you, led you half-hypnotized where she wanted you to go. Like a conjurer she kept us busy, kept us interested, kept us occupied, kept us fascinated, winding us in endless strings of reciprocal talk, ropes of argument, singing necklaces, bracelets of laughter, looping us with garments of language, bejewelling us with glittering sentences, bubbling and streaming ideas and thoughts and discussions and exhortations and moralizings, and sometimes, when we'd briefly slipped the spell, an anxious crying of our names up and down the block, or a stern motherly shout or two. Will I ever forget the parrot at Assiniboine Park, who took up and carried on her cries of "Harry! Harry!" when my big brother wandered briefly out of sight one rare holiday afternoon? The very birds of the air seemed to be in league with her.

Not until I heard her with her grandchildren did I remember the feeling of it, those invisible, constantly re-forming bonds which at the same time were roads to explore, teasing us along avenues of thought and imagination. Even now she counsels tirelessly, "You have to talk to children, you have to tell them all the time, explain to them, entertain them, make them understand." I see my daughter following her about with my own mesmerized eyes. I feel the persuasive murmur engulfing me from the past, a haze of language enveloping the enchanted child.

Mind you, even as a child you knew you were being led, and as you grew older you sometimes suspected you were being taken, but who could resist? Who wanted to miss anything? You knew she was building a glittering web to contain you but you knew you were always at its centre, and it was a throne, a chariot, as it became a rocket ship for her grandchildren, perhaps, and she might be controlling you but she was also completely at your service, helping you to learn to work the controls that would take you farther, she promised, than even her dreams. She was artist, magician, slave and seer, counsellor, songbird, judge and peer.

Would you like to see bobba take a bath? she asks her two-year-old granddaughter, reciprocating graciously a privilege received. The child watches while bobba prepares her bath and divests herself of her clothes. A round, white, plump little seal-like creature emerges. She displaces an admirable volume of water.

Baby wash bobba? suggests Tamara, hopefully.

Bobba hands her a bit of soap.

Wash hands?

Bobba holds out a hand. The child gently soaps a patch.

Wash foot?

Bobba raises a still shapely white member.

Wash face.

A cheek is held close.

Wash tsuts! instructs the child.

Bobba manoeuvres one of her plump pancakes within reach. The child works seriously, laving patches of her grandmother's anatomy, which bobba brings to her on command.

Finally, *Wash toosy?* says the baby. Whereupon grandma heaves herself up and around, with a great sploosh, and balancing on one set of fingertips and one set of toes, presents the baby with a small, glistening white buttock.

No wonder we were incapable of conceiving her separate life. She was simply a part of us, as much of her as we could get. Mama with a personal life? Even now, when she sometimes mentions, casually, what I suddenly realize must have been a painful personal crisis that had taken place during those intimate years, I am somehow surprised to hear of it. Hadn't she spent her life at the sewing machine, or the cutting table, the kitchen sink, the grey electric oven, or the big black wood stove which preceded it, or rushing into the shop to placate a customer when daddy lost his temper and stamped his foot? Hadn't she spent her half-leisure sitting on the front steps with her sewing in her hands and a pocketful of sunflower seeds, buying up the shapely automobiles that pleased her as they passed, and regretting the drunken habits of our chauffeur who still hadn't sobered up enough to bring one of them around from the garage to take us for a ride?

The neighbour gave my little brother Morris a cookie. *Little boy*, she asked playfully, *What are you eating?* Chewing contentedly, he replied, *Mama knows*.

It was years, said my big brother Harry, *before I realized that mama was a woman, that she was like other women. Do you remember those corselets she used to cram herself into, with the bones, when we were going out? Daddy or I used to tighten and tie the laces for her. It's funny, it didn't strike me till not so long ago that she wore them because she wanted to look beautiful and slim, for herself, that she was a female and had a female life of her own, a female vanity. I always thought she was just a mother, all for us.*

For her there had never been a time without children. The eldest of eight who survived at least to adolescence (six are still alive), she would tie the latest baby securely to her hip with one of her mother's shawls, and run out to play. Her sister Rose, eighteen months her junior, preferred the household tasks. "Rose used to polish even the soles of her shoes, and put them up on the mantel." So Rose stayed with my grandmother and helped prepare meals for the workmen, or periodically refinished the walls, with the classic mixture of cowdung and mud, before whitewashing them, while my mother looked after the trussed-up babies.

In those days they used to wrap the baby tightly in a long bandage, a winding string. I always carried a spare with me.

I'd take time out to change the child if he was messy, on the ground, wrap him in the clean length, tie him in my shawl again, stick the dirty wrapping in my pocket, and run back to my game of nut marbles or tippee sticks.

"She was like a good little mother," wrote my uncle Isaac, eleven years her junior, from the Argentine.

"I was fussy about my food," her youngest sister Chana told me, when I was able to rendezvous, briefly but unforgettably with three of her sisters and their two surviving husbands, in Russia a few years ago. "She was the only one who could feed me." Chana was eight years old when she saw my mother last. I spent a whole day and two nights "spaced out," as the kids say, with those myth figures of my childhood magically grown old, and two of them splendidly, uninhibitedly fat. War had widowed my gentle Aunt Chana and life had forced on her enough of far less palatable dishes to reconcile her to food. Polya the proud one, the beauty of the house, more worn than a gentler life would have allowed, still flashed that spark from her dark eyes, still moved her mouth in some undefinable way, feature and expression and vitality combining for throat-catching instants to overrule despairing flesh with a glimpse of beauty that drew my eyes back to that worn face again and again. And Rose, the indomitable Rose, seventy-four when I met her at last, so often the small thorn in my mother's cheerful childhood, tattletale, running to tell my grandfather that mother was at the theatre with her first sweetheart, of whom he disapproved, or complaining to my grandmother that my mother was distributing the bread my grandmother had baked for her, in those hungry days, to all the beggars in the district; Rose, magnificently rotund, reaching about to the ear of my five feet inch and a half, asking now so wistfully after her gifted and impulsive elder sibling. And Rose the cossack at seventy-four, after two sleepless nights and a day, setting out on foot at dawn when we left, to see once more the medical college in Minsk, where her daughter had studied, "because I may never have the chance again."

That Russian visit remains an unforgettable kaleidoscope: of seven adults and two-year-old Tamara stuffing themselves into an eleven-person hotel elevator, and hoping the door will manage to close; of banquetting unbelievingly on cream puffs and Georgian champagne, courtesy of the Russian aunts and uncles; of my large, quiet uncle Josef getting up to make a toast, recalling that my mother had been the one who had matched him up with Rose, for whom she'd fancied him at first sight, and breaking down, finally, in the middle of expressions of affection and gratitude. "What?" cries tartar Rose, "you're crying? I've never seen him cry before!" And sitting quietly on the benches of a shaded boulevard in the afternoon, we talked, exchanging lives, and gazed at each other and briefly, unforgettably, permanently interlocked worlds, while wiry, lively uncle Shura, Polya's husband, played with the child, and I marvelled at the deep resemblance in the bone between my mother and Rose and between Polya and my Winnipeg aunt Sonia and between myself and them all.

You really saw my little sisters.
> *Yes mama. Look at the pictures.*
> *But Rose was a beauty. How could I ever come near her? When did she look so much like me? And Auntie Sonia and Polya. How do they come to look so alike? Little Shura. They were our neighbours on the same big yard. I remember only a dark, handsome little boy with big eyes and always a snot like a yoyo. Josef, the minute I saw him, I knew he was for Rose.*
> *Polya doesn't remember she didn't want Rose to be courted by Josef. When I reminded her of what you said about how she climbed up on the bake oven when he came the first time, and wouldn't come down to be introduced, she said she didn't remember any of it.*

> *And I remember to this day. She was just a youngster, but so proud, so haughty.*
> *She's not haughty any more, mama.*
   My mother's face flushes. Her eyes seem to disappear. She weeps. *The years make fools of us all.*
   Presently she asks, *And they told you what happened to our parents, to Chanaleh's husband, to my brother Sander?*
> *Yes.*

She weeps again. I wait for her to ask for details, knowing I will tell her, but hoping not to have to just yet. I won't refuse to share with my parents the truths, however painful, which they have always respected me enough to share with me. When they dedicated their years to earning, for their children, a choice of futures, we accepted it as our due and our destiny that we were to study and learn and become, and were convinced that not only our own lives, but life itself would be enhanced thereby. Our faith was the more acute for our awareness of the alternate, simultaneous fate of our helpless counterparts, the Jews of Europe. The gift of choice, under these circumstances, takes on an almost religious significance. I took my own destiny seriously, an attitude which retrospect always discovers to be more than slightly comic. Equally serious about the fate of our six million, I have found that time has left no leavener here. I know that I must pass on, eventually, both to parents and child, my few garnered details of the deaths of my grandparents, or deny the reality, the shape, the dignity, the great mystery of their so savagely truncated existence. But some endings are hard to lay on those you love.

Not that my parents are strangers to violence. What could I tell my mother that she has not already known in one form or another? Even her nostalgia sits childlike amid the rubble of human stupidity and destructiveness.

On the first day of the pogrom they razed a neighbour's shop. The next morning my friends and I slipped out of ur family hiding places and got together to explore the ruins. There was only a deep pit left. But such treasures in that pit! Buttons and bits of glass and scraps of this and that. What more do little children need? Our parents finally found us down there hours later. By this time they were frantic. The pogrom was not yet over. At any moment the hooligans would be back. Mama smiles reminiscently. *Such pretty bits of coloured glass.*

We are walking along the street. My arm hovers solicitously, in case she should need help, or want to lean, as an old woman may. Suddenly, she darts forward, stoops swiftly, straightens, holding a partly squashed tin button. "I could use this somewhere," she murmurs, tucking it away.

———————————

Since their children have grown up and have gone their various ways, my parents have been on a many years' routine of visits, often in response to emergency calls for help, from all around the continent. They have become quite sophisticated about railway stations and planes and airport limousines. In their absence, the little house on Burrows Ave. has been burglarized four times. Oh to have been a fly on the wall to watch even one of those felons, eager for the illicit profit of his form of free enterprise, as he rushed from room to room, wrenching open drawer after drawer, and turning out the zipper heads, the spools, the bottle tops, the springs, the plastic lemons and limes, the thousands of bits of gaily coloured cloth, of fur and feather, the buttons and sequins and ribbons and leather, the foam rubber, the shells and coral and stones and expended flash bulbs and thread and wool and junk jewellery and broken trinkets. I did, as it happened, arrive on one such occasion, on time to see her treasures littered about the house. What could that burglar's reaction have been to the carefully scrubbed and dried soup bones and fish spines and curiously shaped wood and dried leaves and odds and ends of every kind of discard imaginable? My mother's collection of treasure is enough to challenge a whole system of values at a far profounder level than any mere burglar can manage.

Nothing is wasted, nothing is cast aside to lead a used-up, fragmented, uncreated existence. Everything is suggestive; everything is potentially a part of something else.

> *Pieces of material when they lay around they bother me, because I want them to look like something.*

buttons (glass, tin, plastic, leather, all kinds)

sequins

cloth materials (cotton, silk, lace, velvet felt, wool, denim, synthetics, plastic, all kinds)

fur, leather, leatherette

ribbons, ties, bows

pipe cleaners

styrofoam, plastic, vinyl

cardboard (cutouts from boxes, e.g. dog biscuits, wine, cereals)

lemon squeezes, lime squeezes

nylon stockings, socks

onion bags

yarn, thread, wool, string, twine, all kinds

lids and caps from spray cans, shampoo, perfume, bottles,

stoppers from perfume bottles

plastic centres from rolls of tape

feathers, pom-poms

snaps, hooks and eyes, clips, clasps,

pull tabs from zippers,

costume jewellery:

pearls	beads	charms
bracelets	fake watches	
necklaces	real watches	
rings	pendants	
earrings	small bells	
pins	badges	

elastic ribbons

toys

plastic pieces from building sets, plastic rings, prizes from popcorn boxes, aluminum pielet plates,

bottles: wine, shampoo bottles, dropper bottles, yoghourt and sour cream and cottage containers, soya sauce jugs, liquid soap bottles, "bleach" jugs and bottles, medicine and liquor

fish bones: spines, tails, fins, shark teeth, bear teeth

frog legs

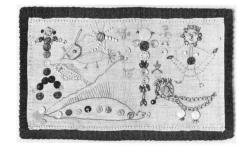

eyeglass lens
spools from thread: plastic, wooden, cardboard heads from tacks
pins
buckles and straps
fuses and spark plugs
shells, coral
driftwood, firewood
medals
liquor bags
gloves, mitts
locks
sun glasses' frames and lenses
rolls from toilet paper and paper towels
cherry stems
salmon spinal discs, coony and pike spinal discs, fish tails
turkey and chicken neck bones, wishbones
seeds: melon, orange, grapefruit, lemon
bits of embroidery, dress trimmings, crochet
cow bones, lamb bones
plasticine
button leavings
place mats
ginger marmalade crocks
hospital I.D. bracelets
corn husks
corn silk

AND MORE

Redeemer of waste, champion of leftovers, saviour of non-bio-
degradables, apostle of continuous creation, she has this hunger to
find and establish new relations between things, and so create new
things. She knows that they too will disappear or be destroyed, but

that is not her concern. She knows that somewhere there will still exist this hunger she shares, to make something else again.

The people should feel that even the doll is happy to be created, like I feel.

Her values are impeccable if unorthodox. One of the first junk jewellery pictures she ever made consisted of figures made of sequins and buttons and jet and glass beads and other odds and ends, glistening on black velvet she'd sewn onto a piece of cardboard. The figures seem to come dancing out of the stars.

Mama, I remarked, staring at the silver face of one of them. *Isn't that my Governor General's Medal?*
> *Yes,* she replied cheerfully. *Why should it just lie around the house?*

Even Emily Carr didn't do better when she got her friend to chuck her newly received medal at a dead bird she wanted to shift from the eaves facing the window she had to stare out of during the last few weeks of her life. That medal now makes sense.
More recently, when she heard that a cash prize goes with the

medal now, she remarked, *What, they give you more than a button nowadays?*

She has never made a carbon copy. She has never made two creations alike. That's one of the reasons why the sheer unabating volume of her production is so astonishing. There is something of nature's prodigality, nature's spontaneity, nature's generosity in her output, and nature's sometimes hit-and-miss experimentalism too. Indeed, existing in complete harmony with her Judaism, is an utter faith in and submission to nature, "Die Natoor," as she calls it, and she calls upon it frequently as a touchstone of what is. For nature is that aspect of the unknowable which allows itself to be known; it is divinity revealing itself in action, and man is a part of that revelation, a part which can, to some extent, shape its own contribution to the continuous process. But nature shares responsibility. We were talking about the Nazis the other day, and she remarked, "You think it's all their fault? Nature made them that way." She appears to view evil as a form of crippling.

I put forward these comments as a somewhat tentative interpretation of her preoccupation with nature, and her consciousness of herself as a functioning part and subject of natural process. The point of interaction between all worlds, is, for my mother, the natural world, which, I suppose, is not too surprising, since her history has been a woman's history. Her experience has been the experience of wet hands and working fingers and the incredible earthquakes of birth, and cradled arms and swollen, running breasts, and telling time by when the baby finally stopped crying, and knowing pain as she knew joy, not only within the limits of her own physical being, but as she apprehended them in all of us, the extensions of her being.

Perhaps it is because she has spent so much of herself in direct and very basic existential struggle that she can enjoy the smooth social surfaces with which we gloss our day to day, and completely discount them at the same time. She has achieved a rare kind of liberation from accepted ways of responding, a liberation which both encompasses them and can completely reject them simultaneously. She still takes great delight in beautifully dressed people, but her delight is aesthetic, and impersonal. Her approval does not include a value ticket on the wearer. The more I contemplate my mother, the more I realize that without ever having broken laws, without having openly flouted the ways of men, she is profoundly, unconsciously, but unequivocally, a menace to the cramped and stereotyped ways of the daily mind. "What would I do with diamonds?" she remarked not long ago. And thoughtfully, "I might work them into a picture."

More than once an aspect of her production has forced me to re-examine my own premises. A neighbour of ours had chopped up his Xmas tree for firewood, and stacked it neatly near his door. Mom noticed one particular chunk of wood, with bits of branches sticking out of it, and snaffled it for her own. "I could make something from it." She did, with the help of her four-year-old granddaughter; they busied themselves with creating what I call a "tree of life" and she sees also as a kind of ship, with all sorts of figures attached to it, growing out of it, hanging down from it, tied to it. The bottom branches are covered mostly with cloth cut-outs of curious, slithering, primeval creatures, which gradually evolve to more familiarly suggestive forms, until at the very top a little boy sits feeding a bird. The effect is delightful. Only ... only there hanging from one of the branches is one of my dad's little plastic eyedrop medicine bottles, which in itself would be fine; its shape is pleasant enough — only it's still got the wrapper with the printing on it. It's recognizable. It's identifiable. It's specific. I have never bothered to lean over and read which drug house it comes from, but I could. Why does this cast a mote in my aesthetic eye? Why did I try, in a roundabout way, to get her to take the offending bit of paper with the writing on it off the little bottle? I desisted when I realized she felt it was just fine that way, because I recognized I was on the verge of behaving like an editor. Similarly, she doesn't bother to take the labels off the liquor bottles she turns into dolls, or the soap and bleach and soya sauce jugs. She simply

incorporates the strange writing and elaborate logos into the over-all effect. She cuts the pictures off cereal and other boxes and makes mobiles with them. I find myself admiring her ingenuity but repelled by her materials. I ask myself, finally, why?

I suppose the answer is that I too am involved in the ambivalent product-consumer romance continuously being re-enacted in our society, in which the company with something to sell sets up the product as the seductive maiden; the public is ardent young manhood, and the advertizer is pimp. Young manhood is dazzled by pimp's packaging of young maiden, buys and uses said maiden, and comes away "*triste*," feeling somehow cheated, obscurely aware that he has perhaps got something other than he's bargained for and certainly less than he's paid more than he can afford for. But now maiden is gone and only package is left to be tossed out in the gesture of residual resentment. The whole performance is replayed constantly, as part of the rhythm of our existence, just as the knight in the classic erotic metaphor rises but to fall again. Pop artists, in recent years, have tried to place these objects of ambivalent consumer eroticism before the public eye with didactic intent. My mother is innocent of these considerations. She sees the object itself, its shape, its form, its possibilities, in another context. She does not know that it is part of a "sell." She does not know that it is culturally and economically fixed in a seduction-degradation formula. Somehow she has escaped the guilt of this particular kind of self-betrayal-self-disgust of our time. To her it is all equally real, the interesting aspects of the box legitimate in themselves for consideration in other contexts. Her eye, in its innocence, redeems instantly all the actors of this characteristic contemporary performance, in a way that only time could otherwise do.

Regardless of the aesthetic success of any particular object my mother produces, I know her attitude to be a purer one than my own. If I were to stow away carefully some of those product wrappers that I now hasten into the fireplace, and were to wait for fifty years or so to bring them out again, they would have lost, by then, their current emotional heat, and would emerge in a glow of nostalgia, to be sought after by collectors as objects of kitsch and souvenirs of history, and even, in some cases, as "ART." All this is to say that another culturally determined attitude would be brought into play toward my erstwhile reject. I compulsively pick up all kinds of "old" junk myself, simply for its oldness, its frozen bygone stance. My mother is far too much of a "maker" to be bothered by any of these considerations.

Pictures? It amazes (amuses) me. Why should junk lay around and not be used? I start with heads and junk and make little chains, and so on, and they make out pictures.

When you begin, do you know what you're going to make?
> No. I take a piece of cloth. In my mind I'm happy.

She doesn't know that you're not expected to feel with your mind, nor think with your hands. She is all of a piece, and accepts what is, her mind forefeeling the wholeness that is to be, foretasting fulfilment, her fingers ready to shape a future, teasing it from the cloth, the zipper ends, the eyeglass lens, the spools, the springs, the flotsam of possibility. Every creative act begins as a foray into chaos. The raider submits to the alien dimension. Function is disrupted. Possibilities are fluid. To some, as I have already mentioned, it is an intensely terrifying, if compulsively necessary experience. There is always the danger of total surrender, disintegration. Simultaneously, however, the creator feels herself to be in a state of pregnancy, knows the acute conviction that she is on the brink of a new and meaningful order. Sometimes an extraneous upset provides the preliminary emotional shaking loose:

> *It's a funny thing, when I'm very upset about something I do my best work. I get so many ideas for dolls, for things I would like to make, just when I feel worst. I sit and the dolls fly from my hands.*

Sometimes the breakthrough is achieved during the relaxation of consciousness in sleep. Victory comes too in unexpected guises. The basic structure of the benzene molecule declared itself visually to Kekule in a persistent dream. Einstein sensed the shape of the universe in eye and muscles, traced and symbolized the voluptuous fulfilment of comprehension in crisp, mathematical phrase.

Although she may not have a definite idea always of precisely where she is going at the beginning, mom's choices and rejections along the way make it clear that there is a particular harmony toward which she is groping each time, a definite "feeling" which signals inner success. I once watched her make and attach and remove and remake and attach and remove and remake several times, a little hat for one of two "sister" dolls; each time she muttered, "It doesn't go," or "It won't suit, it doesn't fit," till she was finally satisfied that she had got it right. There was a definite idea at the back of her mind toward which she was groping, and she could not leave this detail until some at least satisfactory approximation to the felt ideal was achieved. What artist has not been forced to submit time and again to this inexplicable but obstinately felt dissatisfaction? As a spectator I couldn't make out what was bothering her, each time she showed me another version of the little hat. Nor was the end result a wildly extravagant example of hatliness in itself. It was an extraordinarily simple hat. But it was just "right." The difference between myself and my mother, in this instance, was that until I saw it I couldn't know what was "just right" for that doll, and mother, of course, couldn't rest for having to know, for having to make known.

I do not mean to assert that there is only one, in every case, absolute right for any particular doll, for I have seen her change the outfits of dolls that have got dirty or tatty, in quite a cavalier fashion, and sometimes over my protests, when it's been a doll I've grown particularly fond of as-is, over the years. Hers is after all a very flexible medium, and dolls, as every small child knows, were made to be stripped and dressed again. But every change she makes has to be "right" too, and conform to some underlying integral wholeness of conception. From one of the big, soft, buttonless dolls that she had made for her infant granddaughter, I removed a colourful tape, which, criss-crossing his chest, gave him a vaguely uniformed appearance. I was afraid the child's tiny hands would get tangled up in it. Several years later, mother picked up the well-used, dirty but cheerful doll, looked at it a moment, and proceeded to replace the tape in the original fashion.

If I'm not satisfied, I re-do them. I like all of them should look
cheerful.
> Do they all?
> Most of them.

That is a statement of a conscious choice of attitude. The dolls are to embody not only an expression of life and about life, but a response to life, a way of looking at life. This is characteristic of art works, particularity of voice of the creator. It is the recognizable result of the integration of complex factors: inherent temperamental disposition confirmed or modified by experience, a way of seeing, thinking, feeling, responding, which disposes the artist to choose what and how to see and so confirm the reality of his inner world, by making it a part of the outer world. There is a particular complex of feeling which satisfies each creator that his note is true. This does not mean, as anyone who looks at the dolls can see, that mother builds a huge grin onto each face to make sure it will look cheerful. It is not pretence, to gloss over reality. It is the choice of what alone can satisfy, as a viable attitude to reality. It is the point of balance, the artist's truth, the personal flush or bias of an art work, the stamp of temperament. It is the vital component of "style." The "note" of an artist, by the way, may not sound the same to his audience as it does in his own head. In that sense, once it is achieved, it is no longer his own, but is part of a separate whole, his product, his gift. What we sense as artistically false is usually an attempt on the part of the supposed artist to create a world of feelings which has no profound base in himself. They are hearsay emotions, wishful feeling. We intercept false tones and fake rhythms. Our distrust reflects the creator's imperfect commitment, his lack of a true note.

Sometimes I think about the background of families that don't
treat children as good as should be done, and I think if they
have nice dolls the children will be happy and forget.

> *Why do you feel you have to make the children happy?*
> *I feel … I feel … there is so much unhappy in the world.*

She appears, at times, to conceive of the doll as a kind of remedial social action, as comfort, as mother, as redress, as a little gesture toward balance, for some child, of its world's ills. I ask myself, "Does she mean art as alternative? art as instrument? art as salvation?" and I remember suddenly and vividly my own utter conviction, from that moment so far back in childhood that I can no longer locate it, when I knew that I was meant to be a writer, that my writing was going to bring truth and understanding and love to the world and make everything and everybody happy and perfect. I remember assuming that everybody else must want to be a writer too, all this in the face of the somewhat puzzling fact that big brother and sister seemed to have equally messianic passion for engineering and the medical sciences respectively, and the further baffler, that little brother did not yet seem to know how he was going to save the world. This sense of significant vocation, felt in varying degrees, this tendency to generalize the potential of inward gifts, is fairly characteristic of people who create, the fall-out of heightened vitality, and is probably part of the necessary motivational push to get them going in the first place. But it is not by any means always at the forefront when they are working. I have found, in fact, that I have usually had to scuttle a beloved didactic purpose before I have been allowed to enter my own new world. If any of it ever surfaces again, it is on the terms set by the logic of this new world, not by fondly held preconceptions of my own.

But the terms of the new world, even when not didactic, can be equally as disturbing to society as direct propaganda, and even more unsettling. Beauty, the aesthetic criterion, for instance, if allowed, can function as a great renewer of human innocence, a redeemer of human error. The artist is more apt to observe nature's possibilities than society's dicta. Among my mother's doll couples, for instance, there is a great deal of miscegenation. She

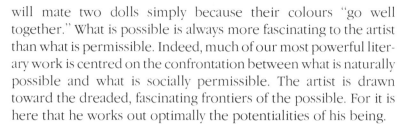

will mate two dolls simply because their colours "go well together." What is possible is always more fascinating to the artist than what is permissible. Indeed, much of our most powerful literary work is centred on the confrontation between what is naturally possible and what is socially permissible. The artist is drawn toward the dreaded, fascinating frontiers of the possible. For it is here that he works out optimally the potentialities of his being.

As we have already seen, culturally unacceptable content can outlive its unacceptability simply by the insistent vitality of its being. That, of course, is why art is so dangerous, always, and why the artist, even in his very innocence, can be dangerous. His aesthetic criteria themselves so frequently contradict vested interests, even when he is consciously of a conservative and even conformist cast. And his product has the temerity to insist on its own validity. Nor is it a quickie in a fancy wrapper which may or may not be tolerable fifty years hence on the nostalgia market. It is true love. It bears repetition. It wears. Furthermore, the artist cannot be trusted to leave well enough alone. He will go on seeing even more. For people like my mother, not only does the emperor have no clothes on, but he has a nice figure.

No wonder society mistrusts the disturbance the creator implies, resists the extension of consciousness that he brings, refuses to comprehend as long as possible, what in the end, can, in fact, bring no small measure of relief. But let a human being once find the freedom and mastery of a language to the extent that he can both lead it and submit to its possibilities, let him but know his need, and he will, whether sophisticated, trained, aware, focussed and ambitious, or naive, innocent and even ignorant of the implications of his performance, be impelled to cast off and set sail along his own singing vein to seek the heart.

We had a very fine dressmaker in our town, Bailka. Once, when I was fourteen, I happened to run into her mother. 'Do you want to be a modistka?' she asked me. Bailka offered me three rubles a year as an apprentice. That would be like three dollars. My father said, 'What? A seamstress?' I was his firstborn, after all, and he was not then a poor man. But I persuaded him. I promised to go on taking school lessons with a private teacher. And I did, for quite a time.

Fascinated by colour, shape, design, the texture and variety of materials, the form of the human body, the flow of movement, the richness of the effects to be achieved by working with all of these, she learned quickly.

I started . . . it took only six weeks, and I bought French batiste and lace, and made myself a beautiful blouse. I was proud of myself, and Bailka was proud of me. By summer she offered me fifteen rubles for the year.

At fourteen also she was playing the leading lady with a group of her seniors, in amateur Yiddish theatricals. She was Yehudas, bride of Uriel d'Acosta, in the play about that precursor to Spinoza in the challenging of orthodoxy. And she was privately tasting the cup of Juliet. High spirited, impetuous, she had already become engaged to "another" to spite "him," and had broken off that engagement.

I lost him anyway. It was my own fault, my own pride. I was too wilful, and I lost him. When you know it's your own fault you must be silent and bow your head.

My mother can humbly bow her head and manage to hold it bloody but unbowed at one and the same time. Once, she nearly lost it.

The White Cossack Captain towers in the doorway.
Does one Sander Rosenberg live here?

Chaika, eldest daughter of the house, replies, *Yes.*

> *Where is he now?*

He knows, obviously. It is pointless to lie. *He's with the Red Army somewhere,* she admits.

> *We've been told that he has arms hidden here,* says the cossack. *We'll have to search the place.*

> *It's not true. You'll find nothing here.* She adds impulsively, *I'll stake my head on it!*

The cossacks search and find nothing. On his way out, the Captain pauses to look down at my mother-to-be, every inch of four foot plus a few, including head. *You know*, he says, *you must never say a thing like that again, no matter how certain you are. If the neighbours were capable of betraying your brother, they were also capable of planting arms without your knowing it. You might have lost your head.*

From which, *He was a good person,* my mother concludes. *He could have killed us all anyway.*

Mother's assessments of people, if sometimes unorthodox, are basically realistic, and tempered with an understanding, and perforce acceptance, of human limitation, of the "shape" of "things." Once, she and a friend of mine were discussing the good nature of a common acquaintance. My friend asked whether mom thought good nature was a quality that was developed in a person or whether it was inborn. "You see in nature there are valleys and mountains," she replied. "You can't expect everything to be even. So in people there are different natures."

Another old friend, a devout and kindly Christian, was looking at a massed display of the dolls for the first time. He noticed that quite a few of them seem to represent Russians or Ukrainians dressed in variations of their characteristic costumes. Obviously thinking of past atrocities and indignities, and my known continued concern about them, he murmured gently, as he eyed her cossacks and peasants, "She's not bitter." I was, as usual, a little startled and

faintly amused. It is a common, and perhaps necessary fallacy of gentiles, in the multiple bind of their relationship with the Jews, that in spite of a history of two thousand years of turning every available cheek to provocation — surely a fairly mild if life-enhancing expression of the urge to vengeance for persecutions sustained —Jews must be vengeful and bitter. If they weren't vengeful and bitter about Christian treatment, wouldn't they embrace the religion that invented love and forgiveness so often revealed to them? Intelligently devout and warm-hearted Christians are particularly touching in their response to signs of lack of bitterness in Jews, not only because of the ultimate conversion-of-the-Jews motif which is doctrinally crucial to Christianity, but because, good human beings feeling themselves implicated, however unwillingly, in the guilt of horrible deeds, they yearn for reassurance that they have not too easily forgiven each other and themselves.

Different world views create different worlds, and we wander as shadows in each other's paths. The fact is that Jews are not theoretically committed to aspire to undertake to behave as gods, but simply as good human beings who love and respect life and the living, an undertaking in which it is as easy to fail as is that of treading the paths of gods, but which has the merit of not being doctrinally doomed to failure. My mother's face is turned toward life, always. The whole question of vengefulness and bitterness, guiltily projected on the Jew from without, is a part of someone else's game into which he is periodically dragged, and forcibly twisted to confront the death which is another's obsession. Given a breather, he buries his dead and turns to life again.

I grew up hearing repeatedly a long list of warnings, and realistic warnings they were too, if some of them did indeed seem far-fetched at times, for my time and place. I cull but a few from a formidable compendium of fears and anxieties, each the souvenir of some particular horror experienced by my mother at first hand. So many things she was afraid of, so many warnings to pass on to us, not to frighten but to alert us, to prepare us.

> *Beware of mad dogs; I was crossing the bridge to Bogopol once with my little dog Moorzik, and suddenly a mad dog appeared and ripped him apart before my eyes.*

And yet, we were never without at least one dog, and at one time we had thirteen cats as well. I find myself passing on familiar warnings to my own child: "Never try to pet a strange animal until you've asked his owner if he's friendly." I too must sound the right note of anxious conviction, for I once heard my not-yet-three-year-old ask a woman, "Is your baby friendly?"

> *Beware of fire; see the scars on my back? Beware of roving pigs. I've known them to eat children in their cribs. Beware of cows. I saw one toss a little girl by her pigtails and rip open her scalp. Beware of outdoor privies; my girl-friend fell in one*

night neck deep. Beware of sunstroke; how they rave with it.
Beware of strange men who offer candy; beware of gentiles at
Easter.

Beware, above all, of human beings, epitome of all irrational forces which can do you harm. My little mother, brimful of all those fears, yet contains them within the larger compass of an undiminished appetite for life, an undiminished zest for coping, and undiminished faith in possibility. It's true, the soldier grabbed her as she climbed the steps of the train, and, though she was very pregnant, roughly threw her from the crowded car and clambered on himself. But didn't a passing officer, noticing, pull the soldier from the train and slap him, and proceed to lift her up and set her back on the train again? Years later, in Winnipeg, in the civilized land, during the depression, she had brought all four of us all the way downtown to the department store where there was a sale on children's socks. Just as she managed to reach the counter and was trying to match up a pair of socks, she was again lifted bodily, swung high, and set down none too gently outside the milling crowd by an enormous woman who then proceeded to engorge the socks. Baffling, pregnant correspondences which trace persistent tracks in the individual imagination, shape the constant questions and the uncertain answers. Once, in the old country, she had slapped and cowed by sheer presence the leader of a gang of local toughs, one of three who afterwards hanged an entire Jewish family. Still later, they themselves were all three hanged by the Red Army. And where are all the many others like them who weren't? Across the street, perhaps, or down the road? Unbearable possibilities to be faced and borne nevertheless. Some people are so badly traumatized in life that they can only seal themselves off from great areas of their own experience, to cauterize their pain, and numb the dread that would otherwise, on encountering a familiar expression in another's eyes, send them raving. But nothing closed my mother off from her own experience, or diminished either her sense of her own essential dignity or her perception of alternate possibilities. It was the fulness of this still-living experience which she offered her children in all its dimensions, open for our exploration, like an extension of our own living space. Because of it our lives have seemed to flow through each other. As a child I haunted my mother's past existence, her generously shared fiefdom, like a ghost from the future. The three towns of her youth, the living source of much of her vision, were the fairyland of my childhood. Hers was another life to play in, an extension of my own through which I could reach into a pre-existence as mysterious and exciting as the ever-redeeming tomorrow in which I would somehow retroactively set everything right. Here I examined clues, discovered correspondences, and listened, hearing, in the shells of her past, the oceans of my future.

I remember how hard I tried to visualize mom's "home," to locate it in what I knew of space. I remember straining to envisage miles of ocean, trying to imagine distance incomprehensible, and finally, in an act of desperate will, "locating" her town, willing it into visual existence in my head, in the vast space I knew best. You went up from the edge of the prairie, over vague tracts of water, on a kind of wooden stepladder to a boardwalk in the sky, and there they were, the rickety wooden houses, the cows, the peasants, the rivers, the grandparents and aunts and uncles, my mother's people, my auxiliary world.

Not far from Odessa, and fairly close to Kiev, in the Ukraine, are two rivers, the Bug (Boog) and the Sinyuha, or Blue River, which meet and run briefly together, parallel, side by side, in the same channel. "Like brother and sister, one red-haired and one brown," my mother explains, "or like Siamese twins," she adds thoughtfully. The Sinyuha is a silvery grey, the Bug a darker, ash grey, and mother says there is a clear line which marks their separate flow, where the two shades of grey run side by side, each within its separate current. They meet and surround a small "pleasure" island, as she calls it, flow together again under a high railway bridge, on the Sinyuha bank of which was, in mother's day, a mill, and on the Bug bank a beer brewery. On the Sinyuha bank was the town of Olviopol, nicknamed in Yiddish Orel. Here, in 1896, my mother was born, Chaia, or Chaika, (a name from the root-form "life," from which "animal" and "pleasure" and "spirit" and "health" also appear to stem) Rosenberg. On the Bug side of the river was the town of Golta, a major rail transit terminus. The rivers separate again to surround Bogopol, or Bapol, an island town once ruled by Turks. Originally, the three towns were connected by ferries, but in my mother's childhood the wealthy merchant (weddings in his family lasted three weeks) who ran the ferries, built toll bridges which were raised when the river iced up in winter.

My father used to build wagons for the brewery. In the summer, we kids would go up to the brewery with a big bucket, and they would fill it with beer.
On the way back the bucket was heavy, and we were hot. So we used to stop every now and then to taste. And we tasted and we sipped, and it lightened the load, by the time we got home.
But, adds mother hastily, and I join her, *YOU NEVER GOT DRUNK ON THAT BEER!*
> *And the fruits and vegetables in that land are bigger, and tastier, and it is not unhealthy to run about there barefoot, as it is here, and the corn is cornier,* I tease.

Mama ignores my callow wit. The fit is on her and she will continue to reminisce in the beautiful, subtle perfection of the Yiddish which is hers and my father's natural tongue. Their English is indeed broken, my father's to the point of fragmentation, because when he could still hear there was no time to raise his head from the machine to listen. My mother is more fluent. For her too English has been a bag of hard nuts to crack, but she communicates clearly, scattering the shells of assaulted language with élan, and often managing to liberate unexpected little kernels of linguistic magic in the process, as when, in making some point about bright stars, one day, she innocently called up "those three wise guys" who followed one. You will have no difficulty here in recognizing when my parents are speaking in English.

> *There was a quiet place where we children used to take off our clothes and bathe in the river when we were small. Further on the horses drank, the women laundered. Some pee, some drink. There was a redheaded postman used to stand high above us on the bank and expose himself to us. We called it the Red Tomcat.*
>
> *And then there were two others, a father and son; we called them the Milkers. Wherever you happened to be, if you looked up, there was one of them standing and milking himself. Both of them, father and son alike. I remember once, a whole bunch of us little girls were playing in the yard, and suddenly, the son appeared. He was a big, strapping boy of eighteen or nineteen. He came running up and grabbed one of my friends, and dragged her off into the barn.*
>
> *Well, the rest of us set up such a screaming and yelling and hollering that he had to bring her back out!*

Shades of all the hen-rooster-fox-and-wolf-barnyard stories I've ever heard. Is that what they're all about? Is this where they begin? We know that parents have a natural impulse to express endearment to their young in animal terms: "My little duck my chickie, my kitten my dove." It is not difficult to see the analogical faculty working, the free movement of the story-making mind developing fable or tale from incidents historic for purposes didactic or entertaining. Anyone who's ever had to put a child to bed with a story "out of your head" will remember how freely we project ourselves and the rags and tag ends of the day's events into animal skin. Our biology may be inaccurate, and our animal psychology all wrong, but then neither are our children that literal minded.

It was a funny thing about the Milkers. The mother too had something the matter with her down there. She had some kind of peeing disease. She had to pee all the time. In those days there weren't many outdoor toilets around, so if you got caught you just found an out-of-the-way place and squatted. Well, wherever you went if they weren't there milking she'd be there squatting. She was really a delicate, refined-looking little lady. In those days the women wore layer on layer of wide, long skirts, so she'd have to arrange the skirts around herself first, very carefully. You'd come upon her arranged like a bell there in the mud, squatting and peeing and groaning.

In the winter the Siamese rivers froze and at Xmas the Ukrainians built fabulous castles and sparkling ice créches that were wonderful to see. And on the river, too, the Jewish self-defence gangs of Golta would have ice fights with the gentile boys who tried to prevent them from skating. But the Jewish boys were tough and well-organized, and they always won the right to skate.

How we skated! We used to form long chains, one hanging on to the waist of the next, and the chain would slither this way and that, and round and round. But I was the smallest and they would always put me at the end. I would be whipped around and around like the tail of a snake. There was a big, dark hole where the water didn't freeze, and as we whirled faster I would be dragged closer and closer to the edge, so that I had to cling with all my strength to the child in front of me. If that chain had broken . . . So many corpses I saw them bringing out . . . .

Past Bogopol, the rivers soon separate for good, the Bug flowing, about thirty-seven verst south, through a small hamlet, Galeskov, or Oleskov, where my father was born, and on to the Black Sea.

The town of Olviopol was inhabited mainly by Jews. Bogopol, a commercial centre, had a large Jewish population too. Golta was inhabited by wealthier gentiles and Jews. It was a centre of culture, a focus of academic interests, boasted theatres, banks, and some famous gentile and Jewish thieves. When they were courting, my parents once walked across the site of what was to be the new "gymnasia," or post-high collegiate there, and mother announced that they could now claim that they had been through college together.

This cluster of three towns, surrounded by gentile villages, was the "home" of which she has always spoken with such longing. Nowadays the whole area is called "Piervomaisk," "First of May," and the three towns are, I am told, one city. We were unable to get to see it when we visited Russia, and of course I know that it is not now anything like the towns my parents remember, or their shadow in my head. But I did get some sense of what it was like when, just a few years ago, we took my parents to the Black Creek reconstruction of a pioneer village, just outside of Toronto. My mother was surprisingly moved. It reminded her of "home." I realized then for the first time what should perhaps have been obvious, that there were many places in the old world that were, at the same point in time, very much like the pioneer villages of the new world. Most people in the world are still, after all, pioneers of simple survival.

How can I explain to my kindly Christian friend that neither vengeance nor forgiveness turn me on the way even the remotest possibility of understanding and comprehension do? So I try to tell him instead something of the language of the dolls because I know and love him and know that this is a language we can share. I wish him to recognize that in a way that has nothing to do with doctrines or with abstract world pictures my mother has conceived this doll person, this button picture, has allowed them their unqualified reality. I draw his attention to the Ukrainian water carrier, and his little peasant wife with the bright, simple dress, that came from leftover scraps of a dress of my own, and the blonde pigtails, and the cloth-covered button eyes that have for pupils two flowers. I talk about how the feeling of great, lumbering peasant is embodied in the form my mother chose for him and the materials out of which she created and clothed him, and in those things as well which she instinctively chose to emphasize. I point out his huge feet in their enormous black clodhoppers, his heavy garments, his thick, dense arms and legs, which are built up of many layers of circles roughly cut out of multicoloured scraps of cloth. This dramatization by emphasis on salient points is characteristic of the naive artist. She is not out to reconstruct precisely, in exact detail, a Ukrainian peasant. She gives us the feel of the man. She creates what she thinks and feels, as much as what she sees.

The cutting of those thick circles alone, by the way, is quite an accomplishment. As befits the characterization, the peasant's arms are rough and craggy. But in some of the dolls the squares and circles are built up in uncanny, smooth, even uniformity. Have you ever tried to draw freehand or cut out a circle? Mother simply holds together a bunch of scraps, in whatever thickness the scissors will take, and unerringly cuts the size of circle or square she wants. She repeats the process again and again to build up arms and legs of whatever degree of uniformity she desires.

As I discuss her work, my excitement grows, and my wonder, and my hope that my friend will find what we are seeing, if only briefly, as liberating as I do. For what the artist creates is consciousness. Hers is an expression of consciousness which extends consciousness. We cherish it because it represents us not as good, but as aware, and lets us feel that we have contributed to the dignity of creation an expression of our awareness of our situation, which enlarges creation and ourselves. This sense of enlargement, of

augmented power, helps us, even, briefly, to imagine that we may somehow become "better."

I cannot resist telling him, though I feel a little silly (but we have so few gifts to give each other), about the peasant who used to bring water up the hill to my mother when she was a young married woman in Golta, during those post-World War 1 years of revolution and chaos, and how one day after she had paid him his kopek she had happened to look out to see him rooting through her garbage, and hungrily devouring the dirty potato peelings she'd thrown out. "How could I leave him that way when I had a loaf of bread?" So she'd fed him, and because of this, and because of the madwoman she sheltered, who helpfully decided, in the middle of the night, to prepare a fire for the morning, and climbed right into the oven, where my mother providentially found her sitting among the kindling she was just about to light, and because of other such incidents, mom's sister had reported to my grandmother that Chaika entertained and supported all the beggars in the neighbourhood.

Rose used to come and help me with my dressmaking. But she never really wanted to learn fine sewing. So I taught her simple things, so she could help me in her way.

Not the way Bailka taught me. With her you had to do a perfect job. If not, pull threads and do it all over again. 'A garment,' she used to say, 'should be so well finished you could wear it inside out.' You would not be ashamed to wear them inside out, those dresses we made, the seams so finely finished. We sewed mostly by hand, in those days, every stitch perfectly even, exactly the same, even the smallest stitches. I loved the fine, fancy work best; the harder, the more complicated, the better I liked it.

We never used patterns. See something original, describe it on paper, come home, mark it out, try after the measurements like I do it now. But fitting is the important thing. I went with

Bailka to customers from the beginning, I should watch and learn. You have to check and recheck. Never wait until the customer finds a fault. You should find it first.

And we designed clothes. We would drape the material on the client in different ways, and together customer and modistka would decide on the style and the effect. We would take into account every aspect of the whole costume, from the type of hat and hairstyle, even to the height and style of the shoe she would be wearing.

Oh I used to love it when a customer would come with an emergency, and we would have to make, out of our heads, a gown for a princess to envy. And for myself? Dancing tonight? How many times out of my mother's lace tablecloth, or a drape, a bedspread, a curtain, anything that caught my eye, drape it, twist it, a flounce, a loop, a pin here, a stitch there, and off I would go, Chaika in her Paris original!

When I make a doll now, it reminds me of when I used to do original dresses on people. I could see it.

Within six months she was a fully fledged dressmaker.

After about two and a half years Bailka got married, and she gave me all her customers. Of course they were very pleased with me. I satisfied them.

False modesty has never marred Clara (the name more suited to the English-speaking palate) Waisman's direct and firm apprehension of herself, nor has insecurity made it necessary for her to boast of her qualities. Early a couple of summers ago, however, she met again, for the first time in fifty-three years, her kid brother Isaac, whom she had left behind in Russia as a boy of fifteen. Isaac had emigrated five years later to the Argentine, to join his sweetheart. Aunt and uncle, now grandparents too, landed first in Miami, where my parents and resident brothers awaited them. I phoned, that first evening, to see if they had actually arrived. My mother brought her unguarded joy to the telephone. "He's just like me!" she cried. "We're cut from the same piece! He's kind and good and gentle and intelligent and unassuming and honest. My little brother. He's just like me! He's so loving and loyal and generous and devoted and good-natured and proud." She kept repeating how just like her he is, reeling off each time a fresh list of virtues and qualities worthy of a whole flight of angels. My nephew and I, listening, nearly two thousand miles apart, were helpless with laughter by the time she paused, simply for breath, not because she had run out of encomiums.

But she is not a crude and competitive egotist in the manner of our time and our culture. "You are best and cleverest and prettiest to me, but there are other mothers, and so there are always more talented children, and cleverer and prettier," she would insist when we children showed signs of incipient vanity. And perhaps that is the way it should be, lest we lose the gifts of admiration, and respect, and the desire to learn, and the sense of our limited place in the scheme of things. This way we lost none of the above, while never fully believing her either.

How often, after an exhibit or a visit to a museum, I've heard her comment, "But there are talents in the world. What am I compared with these?" Once, we took her to the Ontario Science Centre during an exhibition of international crafts, called "In Praise of Hands." Here, in a glass-fronted case she found the work of a ninety-six-year-old man from British Columbia, John Halfyard, a collection of painstakingly handstitched little cloth dolls representing a lifetime of memories touchingly incarnated. Her response was the delight of a creator who, used to working in loneliness, suddenly discovers the work of another such to validate her own intuitions. I've seen young writers "recognize" each other with much the same excitement. Similarly, when she caught her first glimpse of Inuit drawings and stone cuts, "I do work like that!" my mother beamed, delighted that though separated by thousands of chill miles, and different cultures and life experiences and lack of a common spoken language, she and a handful of Inuit artists live and respond similarly in the same real world.

From the real, lived-in world too each generation of creators draws the models for its myth figures. It is common knowledge that Rembrandt sought models for his Christ and his Apostles in the young Jews of his town. So, far less consciously, do human beings of every generation make myths of each other. Get a bunch of North Winnipegers together and let them start reminiscing, and amid the ensuing laughter I begin to wonder, did these people really live? Did I walk among them? Yes, for my sense of my own vitality, of the validity of my existence is somehow contingent on this recognition of them. Somehow the living myths which we are constantly creating, even if only in the most rudimentary and fragmented way, mediate between us and the large abstract and often rigidified myths of our cultures. My mother too has her myth figures, her madmen, her magicians, call them what you will, tutelary craft demigods, clay-sprung like herself, whose gifts she admires, whose pain she apprehends, whose fate she deplores. She has seen living legends, the folk kings and princes of her generation, her walk of life, the kind who bring light and warmth and laughter and even fear, those outraging, outrageous and outraged livers, riders defiantly athwart their own lives, grasping convention by the cold balls, demanding a life larger than life, those heroes persistently and self-destructively and yet somehow redemptively askew.

> *You call me a dressmaker? Oh, I can sew, I don't run myself down, but what's to fuss? We had some, they were known far and wide. There was one, Naftuli Bagalfor, rich people begged him to sew for them. And sometimes he refused.*
> *They called him the drunken master-tailor of Bogopol. He didn't even need to measure. One look and he knew all, how*

much higher the left shoulder was, the hump on the hip, every-thing. He had a shop full of workers. He turned out work that shimmered.

When someone ordered, say, a shiuba, a fur-lined cape, he'd demand so many furs, so much material, and first he would outfit his wife or his daughter. Then if there wasn't enough material left for the actual order he'd demand more. And he would get it. Long before the ordered garment was ready his wife, who was a beauty, would be wearing a gown or a coat or cape or whatever, of the loveliest materials. She looked like a countess. But when he got drunk he used to beat her, and smash all the mirrors in the shop.

He was a small man, but handsome. He had a stick with a gold handle. When he had to bring clothes for a wedding, it was always at the last minute, with the bride already waiting, weeping for her wedding dress. He'd hire three droshkys, one for himself, one for the wedding clothes, and one for his stick. All three droshkys would go racing side by side, and him drunk as an aristocrat, to deliver the clothes when the bride was already practically under the canopy in her underwear. Oh he was famous!

But his daughter went away to America because she couldn't stand the way he treated her mother. And in fact they were relatives of his, young men who had been friends with my brother Sander, who, they said, later told the White Guard that we had arms hidden in our house.

Complex and tangled the skeins of his life, but how necessary an expression to his own time and place and peers was this Naftuli Bagalfor, this supremely fitting, supreme misfit, Promethean of the needle, acting out to its extremes the potentials of his own situation in an imperfect order, turning to deed each wishful, conflicting thought, helplessly wilful maker and destroyer, actualizer of the unbearable incoherence. The comic agon he performed was not only his own. His pre-eminent skill, his smashed mirrors, his contempt for the sacred customer, his golden walking-stick were expressions of the heroic dimension locked in us all. His life revealed and expressed to a generation of humble craftsmen in that distant place their own dreams of defiance and of dignity as their birthright, and warned them, too, of their own fears of so extravagant a breaking of old moulds.

In these stories, and in those I share with the generation of my peers, I recognize like elements, premonitions of meaning, the root stirrings of the urge toward art which we all share. In telling these stories we experience briefly, identify briefly, and then in our laughter, as Koestler has suggested, conquer the impulse to identification, separate ourselves from these acters-out of some-times madly attractive impulses which simply don't go in the world. Normally, we are relieved by this ritual venting, through laughter, of semi-conscious recognition of kinship. But the artist schools himself to seize and hold that instant of recognition beyond the onslaught of laughter. He stays behind to explore the territory implied. His world is resonant with the vital fragments of many worlds. His sacred task is to fish with his fragments on the edge of consciousness, and by compellingly revealing his catch, to make meaning manifest. As her myths and memories urge my mother's fingers, so her dolls and pictures urge me now with the ache of meaning toward the language in which I approximate understanding.

Ours was not the kind of town where anything was allowed to pass unnoticed. Almost before something had happened we already had a song about it running from lip to lip, or a poem the whole town was reciting. No matter how private, how secret: this one's husband had run away to America in the night, that one had been sent off in the darkness to her aunt in another town for an abortion; no one could possibly know about it, and yet by morning the whole town was celebrating.

We had some talented rogues in the place, clever versifiers, no one even knew who they were half the time, but they made something of everything. You had to laugh. You couldn't resist it. You knew you were alive.

Of course the whole district was filled with storytellers. You've heard of Chelm? It was a neighbouring town. And Sholem Aleichem came from another town not far away. And who hasn't heard of Hershl of Esterpol? Another neighbour of ours.

I am struck by the tone of my mother's reminiscences, the emotional quality of the atmosphere in which her life was lived, in which her experiences were interpreted, and to which they were assimilated. It is the tone which permeates her dolls as well. Obviously, it is to a large extent her unique, personal tone. But does it also express something characteristic about the life adjustment of her culture? I caught a glimpse of an answer when I managed to isolate my Winnipeg aunt Sonia briefly, away from her customary routines. A busy, active housewife, one of the few people I know who actually likes housework, auntie lives her life vigorously in the "now." She keeps in touch with distant family by mail, corresponds regularly, unlike my mother, whose correspondence will lapse but who carries her family around with her in a headful of felt presences. My aunt found it difficult, at first, to talk about the past. It is as though life for her has been a continuous process of escape into a present. Persuaded to reminisce, it was with a certain wonderment that she returned to the worlds she had shed. It was only during the early, at first hesitant, steps of reminiscence that she seemed to begin to realize that she had chalked up a life for herself. It struck me as strange that I appear to have been, in some ways, more fully conscious of her than she has been of herself. And yet she is a very intelligent woman. Nor is she a timid lady. We don't run to timid ladies in our family. But it was with a touching timidity that she asked me, finally, whether I thought that even her sons and perhaps their young families might be interested in hearing about her life someday.

My aunt is a very forthright and sometimes a very prickly lady, whom I have always been told I somewhat resemble in character. She will call a spade a spade, and when necessary she will not hesitate to unmask the spade for a pitchfork, though it might happen to be a rake. She is quite different in tastes, temperament and attitudes from my mom. Nature, life and the new world have done different things to her. Her personal note is, in short, quite other than my mother's. Perhaps that is why I was struck when the tone of a culture emerged so unmistakably in her reminiscences too.

We had another little brother. But he died when he was about three or four.
> *What did he die of?*
> *The evil eye.*
> *What?*
> *Well* (slightly uncomfortable), *they said the evil eye. We don't believe in that here, anymore, but in those days I remember that's what they said.*
> *How did it happen?*
> *He got sick and he died.*
> *How did he get it? What did it do?*
> *There was this woman, a neighbour of ours. They said she had the evil eye. I remember mothers always warned their children not to go past her house, especially if they were dressed up nicely.*
> *Why was that?*
> *She'd look at them hard, then, and maybe call them over. I don't know. They say my little brother was all dressed up in a new little outfit, and he went by her place and she must have called him over and looked at him.*
> *But why would she do it? Who was she?*
> *She was a very nice woman, very clean, a good neighbour. And she was good-hearted. She and her husband raised, I*

think, an orphaned niece. But she didn't have any children of her own.

> *Is that why she had the evil eye?*

> *They said. Who knows? In those days they said such things.*
  (It is obvious that in auntie the strength of remembered convictions is at odds with new world "civilized" attitudes. She is at pains to disassociate herself from such stuff. But she is uncomfortable.)
  But didn't anybody ever say anything to her?

> *Oh no! The people didn't want to hurt her feelings.*

> *You mean, she didn't know she had the evil eye?*

> *No. Of course not. She couldn't help it. Of course now we don't believe in the evil eye. But that's how they thought then. And my little brother died. Didn't your mother ever tell you?*

How essentially logical all human theorizing is, once you know its premises and the bias from which it proceeds. It only seems strange and primitive from the point of view of a different set of premises. What is remarkable is the non-punitive tone, the essential compassion of the interpretation. The stories to which mom referred when she spoke of the wise men of Chelm, and Hershl, the wise fool of Esterpol, have running recognizably through the sly humour and self-mockery the theme of essential human helplessness, the imperfect quality of all knowing. The fool is in as direct contact with wisdom as the wise man, and in fact fools can be wise men and wise men interchangeably fools. It is understandable that a society under constant seige should recognize most acutely that we are not in any sense in our own hands. So too in the case of the childless woman whose hungry eyes could innocently destroy your child. Superstitions, perhaps, or unsophisticated clothes for intuited realities of feeling. But think of how many women elsewhere were burned at the stake because of interpretations less compassionate.

When I told my mother, by the way, what her younger sister

remembered of her little brother's death, she said, "I never heard that story. He died of some kind of stomach infection. I think my mother had bought fresh strawberries and he ate too much of them."

It seems to me that however individual her personal note, my mother expresses, in her work, some of the best and most characteristic of the tone of the culture in which she was formed. For the artist is not a freak, an oddity, atypical and apart. He is quintessentially the eyes, ears, voice, the reflection of his culture. Your artist is your culture at its quick. This of course is another reason why his contemporaries will sometimes recoil from him and the skeletons he is impelled to air. I have sometimes known even gifted young artists, still suffering from the "I'll show them I'm special" fallacy, who actually believe that their success of the future will finally prove their superior worth to their contemporaries. They don't seem to realize that the very concept, the very mode of conceiving success, graceless and greedy, reveals how even in this they epitomize their culture and their fellows. Perhaps it is not always necessary for the instrument to comprehend itself.

All summer long my uncle Isaac marvels, *But she remembers everything; all the details of our lives, all the people, all the connections, everything that happened. So many things I had forgotten, so many people, she remembers them all.*
I try to get him to lead me along his own paths through that territory, eager for new perspectives on familiar scenes.
> *I can't remember,* he apologizes ruefully. *The large struggles of my life have wiped out all the details. My life is like a relief map; only the high points and the low, only the general shapes remain with me.*
> *Isn't he clever?* mom whispers to me later. *He still reads, reads, all the time. A poor man all his life, but hundreds of books in his home. And he's so fine.*

All summer she reminds him, coaxing in their time together memories buried, not dead.

> *That it should be so fresh in her mind is a wonder.* He is speaking not only of the fact that an old woman has retained her faculties, but that her memories are dimensioned and alive.

I move about the house, occasionally glancing out to the lawn, where, under a rigged awning my guests sit in the shade, four diminutive old people; mother and father, dad in dark glasses, at 81 recovering from a cataract operation, and my newly arrived, fabled uncle of 68, with difficulty persuaded to ride out the heat comfortably in black flower-patterned shorts, and undershirt. He turns out to be, according to auntie, an utterly doting, possessive husband, who can scarcely bear to have his wife out of his sight, much to her chagrin:

> *He acts as though he owns my body, but how can I fight with him, he's so good to me?*

> *He's grown up into such a nudnik,* mother agrees fondly. *Juanaleh,* my uncle leans forward anxiously, though with a touch of the Latin master of the house to firm up his concern, *it's getting chilly. You need a sweater.*

> *I'm not cold,* says auntie.

> *You are,* says uncle, feelingly.

Auntie Juana rolls her eyes upward, mutters *See?* to mother.

> *You don't know how lucky you are,* says mother. *Mine would watch me turn into a block of ice and if he noticed at all he'd say, "What's the matter with you?"*

They laugh, and their men, noticing, smile indulgently, though with slight unease.

Frequently, my ongoing reverie as I putter about my household tasks, is interrupted by great chortles of laughter, and I am drawn to look again, knowing, with a pang, that I have missed another story; another reminiscence may be lost to me. My mother's sewing is, as always, in her hands. She is talking animatedly, threads her needle without looking as I watch, and as I watch she and my aunt are swept by a fit of giggles. Dad and uncle laugh too, but in their laughter is a trace of embarrassment overcome. It is a risqué story, then, for the men are always more prudish in mixed company.

My father was brought to meet his bride-to-be when she was twenty-three. People told him, "Woo her? That one's a spark for the bellows!" He wooed her anyway, and won her with stories, romances from the vast, eclectic reading of a toil-enforced boyhood, the same stories, I imagine, which we kids used to wait so ardently in the hope he might be home on time to tell us at bedtime when we were very little. From Jules Verne to *A Thousand and One Nights*, my father's repertoire was rich. "I thought he made them all up himself," my mother told me somewhat wryly, not long ago.

Some fifty-seven years later, he still looks at his prize askance at times. Occasionally, there is a confrontation of their private, unmatching realities which is baffling to them both, like trying to make one giant jigsaw puzzle out of two complex ones that are similar in shape and colour and have become hopelessly mixed together. The pieces seem to belong and yet they'll never quite make one coherent whole. But it would take another lifetime to sort and separate them, or perhaps another dimension to reveal their inherent unity. And so they remain, a puzzled but indissolubly married pair. From their occasional tensions of orbit they both retreat to habitual positions of tolerance, my mother murmuring the ancient irony of the dispersion, "Well, it's lasted so long, let the diaspora continue," and my father musing over the paradoxes of victory. Even their arguments confirm to him the wisdom of his choice of wife. For my father considers he did well in his marriage not only because she was the daughter of the relatively well-to-do wheel- and wagonwright of the sophisticated town and he the impecunious lad from the backward hamlet. Father's concept of upward mobility is rooted in a more ancient social structure. In the temple hierarchy my father is a mere Israeli, while my mother is the daughter of a CoYan, descendant of the priestly sons of Aaron. Her volatile temperament is a matter of some pride. What could be more positive proof that she is a direct descendant of Moses, bringer and smasher and bringer again of the Holy Tablets? And who could be more suitable for a man whose given name, in Hebrew, is Pesach, Passover?

> *After we'd become engaged I walked over, one day, from my village, Oleskov, to see your mother. It was during revolutionary times, and I tramped across the fields to avoid the roaming bands.*
> *It was thirty-seven verst (thirty-odd miles), so naturally I was hot and thirsty by the time I reached the outskirts of Golta. There was a little shop there, where they sold drinks. I stopped and bought a glass of soda water. I was just raising it to my lips when SLAP! The glass was dashed from my hands, I didn't even get a taste. And she's standing there with her eyes flashing, 'Don't you dare drink!'*

Daddy shakes his head, chuckling, and rocks to and fro on his heels.

> *I was waiting for him. He was all sweated up. What was I supposed to do, let him get pneumonia and die on me, and disappoint my family? Do you know how many matches I'd laughed away before him? The eldest, and twenty-three already, and finicky yet.*
> *My grandmother was married by the time she was eleven. One day, when she was eight years old, just before Passover, she was down by the river with her little friends. Her father had a mill in a town called Piaterota, that means where the fifth regiment was stationed. The children were washing up the everyday dishes, to be packed away for the High Holidays. Her mother, my great-grandmother-to-be, came down the hill calling to*

her, 'Marjm Hannah, come home, you're a bride!' She started to cry. She didn't want to go. She wanted to stay and do her work and play with her friends. So her mother took her by the hand and brought her to meet her future father-in-law, who was a business acquaintance of her father's.

As soon as my grandfather Sander reached adulthood, right after his Bar Mitzvah, they were married. He saw her for the first time when he raised her veil under the canopy.

Luckily, she was a pretty little thing, even as an old lady. They had eight children. My father was her youngest. But my zeida Sander died young. That's why my father had to learn a trade, which was a great blow to the family dignity. My grandmother lived with us for the last thirteen years of her life. She was such a delicate little creature, with her hair drawn up in a tiny little knot. When she arrived at our place, before I was born, she announced that she was eighty-seven years old. After that, no matter when you asked her, till the day she died, she remained eighty-seven years old. I don't know how long she'd been eighty-seven before she came. She must have been well over a hundred when she died. But she died so quietly. One day she was sitting and resting outdoors, and she called me to her and asked me to bring her a glass of varenieh, jam syrup. When we found her dead she was still sitting, leaning, with the glass of varenieh in her open palm.

When we returned from the holy field where they buried her, my father went to the rack where her clothes were hung, and he went down on his knees by her clothing and wept, 'I've lost my mother.'

Not that she had made life easy for my own mother. She was difficult, but my father honoured her, and my poor mother knew how to keep her own lips pressed together.

My dad has moved off. At the mention of death he moves out of range. It is a troubled topic between them. The great tug-of-war over my mother's dead body has been going on for years. Long ago, she began to warn us that she would not be with us in the flesh forever. I suppose she knew this was a necessary part of our education in reality. We responded by teasing her. Who wants to think of those things? "Kicking the bucket again, are you?" was gradually abbreviated to "kicking already?" or whatever variations sprang to mind to deflect a mood which I, for one, was not willing to entertain. But mama made plans. She did not intend to remain idly passive in the matter of the disposition of her remains. Young girls dream romantic dreams of handsome lovers, and mama's romantic dream simply evolved and changed according to her unerring intuition of seemliness. She wanted to continue to serve, she wanted to be needed, she wanted to be useful down to the last cell and corpuscle. Somewhere there must be a young medical student, poor but ardent to be of service to mankind. And what if he were too poor (she knew all about poverty) to be able to afford a cadaver of his own to dissect? How would he learn? How would he make his discoveries? What a team they would make!

When I die I want to donate my body to medical research.
> *Okay, mama.*
> *What's the use of lying around under a stone? You hear me, Peisy?* She raises her voice to catch my father, who paces the house, easing his troubled legs. *Peisy!* Her voice penetrates his deafness and he pauses enquiringly. She repeats her decision, explaining till his large dark eyes grow round and troubled. He shrugs his shoulders, and throwing her an astounded glance, resumes his pacing. *He doesn't like to hear about death,* she says. *Why?*
My father has returned and stands before me, a slight smile on his face.
> *When they first brought me to see her they warned me, 'Why, you won't even know how to carry her parasol to suit her.'*
Chuckling, he wanders off again through the house. Soon he

is warbling away, creakily, one of the favourite songs of his youth.

> *And afterwards I want to be cremated!* she calls after him. *He's afraid. What's he afraid of?* She tosses her head. *There's no forever.*

It is strange that, of them all, my father is the only one who still sings, all the time. For he actually lost his singing voice and the possibility of ever becoming a cantor, during the First World War, long before I was born. On one of the Northern fronts, in dead of winter, he and another Russian soldier were ordered to spend the night hastily erecting a snow hut for a visiting conference of officers. Whatever it was that subsequently ravaged his lungs and bronchi left behind that rasp in his vocal chords. But dad has never lost the cantorial urge, and though he seldom converses, his presence is proclaimed by that continuous, reedy utterance. Maybe his deafness smooths and rounds the sounds inside his head. But there is also something externally compelling in that melody-yearning quaver. I have a tape of my dad passionately uttering one of his favourite ballads into the microphone. As he sings his year-old granddaughter, who has hitherto managed only a step or two, suddenly stands up and totters toward him. The recording is punctuated by my own ecstatic cries as I count her seven steps into his arms.

For all that the mention of death is distasteful to him, my father has on occasion not hesitated to volunteer his measurements for the grave. Curiously, in the pocket epic of his life, which he is always willing to share with you, these incidents are seldom given prominence. It is not necessarily only personal modesty, but a difference in culturally conceived attitude which sees the aggressive masculine display of "guts" as of minor relevance in defining the heroic encounters of life. It is mother who recites the story of another of my father's "walks."

> *We were not long married. We had gone to live in Oleskov, your father's hamlet. The country was in turmoil. The Tchekists, Petlurovtses, Denikintses, Kozakov and his gang, all the murderous bandits were roaming the land. We got word a pogrom had broken out in Orel. I was frantic. I wanted to set out myself to find my parents. It was midwinter; the fields were deep in snow. I was pregnant. Your father wouldn't let me go. He went himself. I let him go.* Mama pauses, appalled.
> *What we do to each other! He tramped across the fields. He walked all day through deep snow, in frost of thirty-five, thirty-seven degrees below zero.*
> My father, head closely inclined, has been listening.
> > *Your grandparents were surprised to see me,* he remarks. *They were barricaded behind shutters in their house, in the dark. They crawled about the floor, with a bit of oil and a thread in a hollowed-out potato, for light. I stayed with them for a week. When it quietened down, I walked home to Oleskov. It was so cold that when he arrived the piece of bread he'd brought along to eat on the way was still frozen in his pocket. And there we were, ready to run. We'd heard there was going to be a pogrom in Oleskov.*
> Daddy laughs.
> *I stopped them. No more running for me. I said 'I'm staying here.' And I went to bed. It turned out to be a false alarm, that time. But in Orel there had been seventy people killed.*

Where did all the singing go? In the first few years of my life my parents and their immigrant friends were always singing. They were not very prosperous, and certainly not always particularly happy. My mother, for instance, was terribly homesick for the old country and her family there. But her light soprano filled our home. And I can still hear my Auntie Sonia's rich mezzo belting out "Oa Chi Chorrrnia!" — Black Eyes Shining Bright, and the sensuous rolling of her R's in the wine velvet of "R-R-R-R-R-Ramona!"

Perhaps it is a trick that time plays, but it always seemed to me that the general singing, that particular youthful gaiety of the grownups, like the excitement of making Kosher for Passover, stopped very suddenly. The great discussions and even hot arguments over whether a trilight lamp or an ornamental rug would be preferred as a communal gift at somebody's surprise anniversary party, and the elaborate plans to ensure real surprise, these still went on, but now they usually didn't bother to bring along somebody's big brown victrola in somebody else's wagon. Now when they came together they formed small groups at small card tables, hunched over in the worship of playing cards. Their fiercely concentrated relaxation briefly held all the other anxieties in their lives at bay, until a squabble broke out. Unravelling nerves already strained by the day, and exacerbated, perhaps, beyond endurance by the loss of a few pennies they could ill afford, husband would turn on wife, sister on sister, kin on kin, and best friends would reveal unsuspected depths of mutual loathing. Those who didn't happen to be in on the fighting had their floorshow for the evening, and the indiscretions of the card table made the rounds of friends and acquaintances for weeks. Of course, there were those who won consistently, and to whom the tables became a tolerable living supplement during those depression years.

My parents weighed up the possible loss to their children if either of them became addicted to the card table, and agreed to stay away. It was a harder choice for my father, I suspect, because my mother was interested in talking with people, and was bored by the endless repetitions on one theme which began to characterize the outlook of the table. Its adherents no longer seemed to her to have any conversation. But my dad would probably have been just as happy with the indirect social contact, and he was good at games. Nevertheless, he refrained, and their social life shrivelled. Perhaps that is why I am still so moved to hear him singing.

Though mama did at some point stop singing, her music did not go away. I am surrounded by music-makers as I write. Here is the elegant green velvet gentleman with the tall, creamy fur hat, whose lighter green arms are joined by a matching creamy hand organ, (originally a plastic spool of some sort). Or again here is the also elegantly accoutred (a symphony in browns) mandolin player, embracing his light cardboard and green thread mandolin expressively, if upside down.

Conductor Sevitsky, who in life used to conduct the Miami Symphony Orchestra, in dollhood conducts my typing. He gazes at me with a slight enquiring smile from coral lips and gleaming jet eyes. Impeccably dressed in black tails, with elegant tape down his pant legs, a white shirt, black bow tie, silver watch chain, top hat, jewelled matching buttons and cufflinks; about sixteen and a half inches from pumps to topper, he conducts with an ivory toothpick the orchestras of remembered visits to her sons.

I gave him hair like Toscanini. Conductor Sevitsky was balder. But he looks nice this way.

As a functioning part of nature, mother likes to help nature along. She is not merely doing a portrait of Conductor Sevitsky; she is helping to give ideal form to one who is still, in terms of what she perceives of the logic of his being, in flux. She is making him more what she sees to be "himself" by adding an aesthetic and cosmetic dimension, in a sense, idealizing him by making him not only Sevitsky, "a" conductor, but Toscanini-Sevitsky, "the" conductor. So most creators try to achieve through "a" man, "the" man, through a choice of particular details the universal resonance.

Mrs. Sevitsky, the conductor's wife, a regal-looking lady, plays the harp. When I brought the dolls to Winnipeg mama would not let a by-now somewhat tatty Mrs. Sevitsky go on stage. She was completely re-outfitted in a restrained but shimmering blue gown, from beneath which depend her long legs in lacy white pantaloons. "But where's her harp? Didn't I make you a harp?" Since there was no time for elaborate harpmaking, she seized what was to hand. Out of a plastic egg carton and some plastic straw tubing she swiftly contrived a strung object. "Of course," she explained, "it's only a symbol of a harp."

That's when I realized that many of the assumptions which we make about primitive or innocent artists, that they are ignorant, for instance, about such things as symbolism, and create unrealistic looking work simply because of lack of craft, are based on our own ignorance of their premises and conceptual framework. My mother, like the most sophisticated, can will a non-representational object to carry a message, whether or not she is actually capable of or even wants to reproduce in photographic detail and dimension the object symbolized. Here again our attitude to education, compulsive tidy-mindedness, serves to limit our perceptions and rigidify our concepts. The ability to symbolize is a function of mind, not education. A concept can be used and understood without being named. In fact the act of naming, with its implication of control, often serves to narrow our comprehension by artificially limiting it. By naming something which might disturb us, we can turn away from it quickly, without having to know it.

Certainly, in some cases of clearly attempted representation, some of the charm or fun of good innocent art is in the way it carries off and in a sense transcends its near misses. Lack of representational skill may determine the limits of expression sometimes, but it is not always the overriding determinant. It may force the artist to find a new mode in which his very lack of formal training becomes part of the particular triumph of his expression, or becomes simply irrelevant, as he invents his own effective

medium. After all, Mrs. Sevitsky's head is made of an empty plastic lemon, covered with a veil of red net from a plastic onion bag. Mrs. Sevitsky's eyes are black-rimmed brilliant-set buttons. Mom did not imagine that she was creating an exact likeness. It was not the desire for simple likeness which determined her choice of materials in the first place. Of course she has great respect for anyone who can produce a real likeness, the exacter the better. I have seen her take delight in what to me was the most execrable pedestrian stuff. She in no way consciously rebels against common standards of "prettiness." There is room for all in her world. But something in her simply by-passes them when she sets out to do her own thing, though mind you if you hand her a vacuous, naked little plastic doll and ask her to dress it in an elaborate costume dress, so that it can reign during the day on your fancy bedspread, mama will do it, beautifully, and enjoy doing it too. She'll even make you the fancy bedspread. She's done both often enough professionally, in her career, for at one time the exquisitely costumed doll on the bedspread was very fashionable in some circles.

But all that is a far holler from the bedspread doll couple she handed me recently, to go with the new purple and print bedspread she had made. The girl stands, built around an empty plastic detergent jug, dressed indeed very prettily in scraps left over from the bedspread. Within a dimple to the right of her mouth sits a black beauty spot, mother's characteristic grace note, one of the personal touches which effectively "dates" her, a lingering aesthetic assumption of her girlhood which is almost a trademark. All in black print and pinks and purple, with clashing, tier-fringed mouth-puckering hair in orange wool, and hat and dress be-silver-sequinned, the doll has something about her of the look of an Ophelia who has decided to delay her dip and give HIM another chance, and who can resist her? Certainly not her "cavalier," as mom calls him, who sits tucked up against her skirt, his large, golden hands clutching an abstract shape clearly suggestive of some musical instrument, "a harp or a guitar or something," she is willing to let the viewer name it. It is attached to a pink and red candy striped shoestring which is secured around his neck, and highlights the sober black of his doubleknit jersey suit, which, with a bit of tasty pink cross-stitching blends in with the black and pink dominants of her outfit. In the scrubbed meat bone which forms his head, hoicks up his left shoulder, and gives his back its distinctive hump, mom has perceived a man of character. How to describe the effect of that long, twisted narrow ivory sweep of the nose, the outflaring curve from under the blue sequin nostril which somehow suggests the long curling line of a lip, eyes also keen blue sequins, and high brows of two little black sequins each? A wide blue headband, crown like, circles the lower promontory of his forehead, and matches his shoe flaps as well as his eyes and nostrils. "He reminds me of the Hunchback of Notre Dame," mother murmurs admiringly.

My sister has another splendid doll and bedspread combination. Hers, in red, white and blue, is a magnificent Garden of Eden, inhabited by a gorgeously accoutred Eve, between whose knees clutched securely, an elegant Adam reclines. Precise instructions for positions came with the dolls. Camouflaged in brilliantly patterned material, a most seductively flamboyant serpent lurks ostentatiously. One of the oldest of the dolls, a red velvet devil gloats cheerfully over the archetypal domestic scene.

Clearly it is not the desire for conventional prettiness, or for simple photographic effects which determines this creator's choice of materials. Mom is moved, in her impulse to visual imagery, by what I call the urge to metaphor. There is a definite idea of what, for instance, the elegant harpist Mrs. Sevitsky is like, which does underlie the choice of every detail. The egg-carton harp has long since gone West, and on a recent visit mom noticed that the doll was once more harpless. So she proceeded to supply a paper and gilt harp, once again a symbolic, mind-patterned harp, in which neither size nor dimension nor precise shape are other than aesthetically relevant. What matters is seductively communicated essence or felt idea. My mother would be kind to you if you commiserated with her on the fact that her portrait dolls don't look like photographic copies of their namesakes. She'd probably hasten to explain that she's uneducated, that she never learned to draw. What she'd be too polite to say would be "What does it matter here?" or, as she would be more likely to put it, with a slight shrug, "Noo?" She too, in her humility, puts a lesser value on the products of what she believes to be her lesser education. Still, it is puzzling that though she makes no claims, you should make demands. The security which we get from accepting unquestionably one set of premises and their artistic and cultural spinoffs, has its negative aspect in tending to reduce our ability to meet on its own terms another set of premises and its concomitant spinoffs. Wasn't she careful to make her Tiny Tim as smiling and bushy moustacheod as the original? Didn't she contrive for the minutely sewn leather nose to be as long and threaded looking as that of its T.V. entertainer original? When she sees him at my place doesn't she always check to make sure that his nylon stocking curl forelock falls just so, and always over his left eye? And isn't he as gaily dressed and sassy looking as an old, cut-off bleach jug can be? If pushed further, she might, to keep you happy, agree that maybe he still doesn't look exactly like THE Tiny Tim. She'll even tell you to call him something else if you like. Privately, like any creator, she may be briefly touched by despair, but will recover to deplore, fleetingly, your lack of vision, or, if you have been rude or condescending, pity your narrowness of space, for there is a limit to what can be excused on the grounds of superior education.

Because the things she produces are charitable in intention, often delightful, and apparently harmless, her activity has a way of infiltrating, at least peripherally, the consciousness of those who come in contact with her. When they realize that she makes things from scraps and leavings, people tend to save for her those odds and ends which they feel vaguely guilty about having to throw out.

My sister knows someone who knows someone who has a plastic button-making factory. Apparently the buttons are punched out of sheets of plastic. There are a lot of oddly shaped little plastic stampings left over from this process. A bag of these found their way to my mother, and shortly after, I received a familiar telephone communication: "I'm making you a beautiful picture. A harpist, but what a harpist; such a picture like you've never seen yet." Harpists at work seem to have a special attraction for her. I respond with greed informed by long sibling experience.

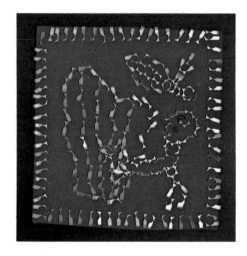

Remember it's for me then. Don't let anyone else talk you out of it.
> *So if someone else gets it it's close enough.*
> *But you said you're making it for me.*
> *That doesn't mean you should grudge your own sister.*
> *So why should she grudge me?*
> *Who says she's grudging?*

This is mama's signal to go off into the lament about how the one thing she's always wanted is that her children should live in amity, not in rivalry and envy, like some. Having invited it I must wait it out, until finally, "Hey, ma, remember the picture you were talking about, the one you're making for me? The harpist? Don't forget, you promised it's for me."

"Wait till you see it." She is tactful but will not be further pinned down. The fact is she sometimes forgets in these later years, and is a little afraid.

The windowlight gleams on the mother-of-pearl plastic leavings as I write. The harp soars upwards above the harpist whose hands, at the end of long arms, create busy clusters at the strings, and whose tilted head and face follow the rising line of the harp. There are only three bits of embroidery in the picture, a black threaded eyebrow, a red threaded growing circle cheek, and, outside the profile of the face, a curiously Picasso-like red bow of lips, also tilted upwards. Balancing harp and harpist in the corner above hangs a fish-shaped chandelier. When she did, at last, give me and none-else the picture, mother handed me a little bag of additional plastic leavings. "They're hard to make fast. They'll fall off easily, and maybe break," she explained. "So you just sew others on."

My mother's enforced apprenticeship to the sewing craft lasted till she was in her turbulent early fifties. We had been evicted from our original shop, when the city health authorities, coincident with the desire of our landlord to break our lease, suddenly discovered that we had been living, for the past six years, in conditions detrimental to our health and welfare. Frightened that with the move we'd lose most of our customers, for poor people wouldn't want to add carfare to the cost of minor alterations, my dad took my adolescent brother Harry, a weightlifter in glowing health, superb of chest and thew, along with him to City Hall to plead our case in English. Of his first vain encounter with officialdom, Harry told me years later:

*I'll never forget the expression on his face when I tried to exp-
lain; the way he looked at me ... that was when I decided that I
was going to do something with my life that would make it
impossible for his kind ever to have power over me again.*

He has been battling bureaucrats ever since.

We moved, and moved again, the Inkster Tailors relocating ever
southward along Winnipeg's Main Street. We were living once
more in mother's by now somewhat battered and silk-fringe-
windowblindless dream house. My parents commuted daily to the
shop. Still an ever-present mother, she did the housework, pre-
pared our meals, and saw us off to school, and then high school,
and finally university, before walking, and later taking the bus or
streetcar to carry my dad's lunch to the shop, where she would
remain to the end of their long evening.

During the Second World War, textiles and trimmings were strictly
rationed, and when my dad was approached as a possible outlet
for a booming black market he opened his glowing brown eyes
wide, pursed his lips and stamped his foot on the new prosperity
of the graveyard. So we were by-passed by that economic lift which
always makes a virtuous war doubly worth having somebody fight.
My parents spent the war years taking apart the uncleaned old
clothes left behind by warrior sons and husbands, and remodel-
ling these to fit wives and children living on war-work wages and
soldier's allowances. To eke out sparse pickings dad worked as a
furrier as well. The two of them laboured on, in their nostrils the
reek of animal dye and damp hides being stretched, and the long-
trapped stench of men sometimes already, or soon-to-be dead.

For us the depression continued long after the war. But by now we
children were nearly grown. My mother had been physically ill;
she was tired. And the work was not coming in, though they still sat
long, hopeful hours in the room high above Portage and Main, in

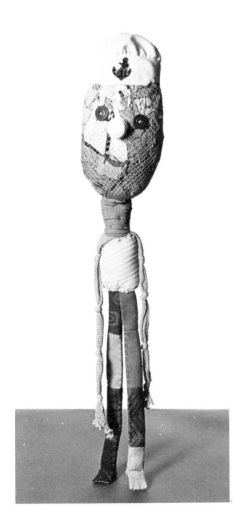

the old McIntyre Bldg. Several times she found herself awakening from some deep reverie on streetcar or bus, to find that she had missed her stop, and had been carried miles beyond her destination to utterly strange parts of town. She became frightened. Finally, she allowed herself to recognize that she could no longer bear the shop. My father, who was by now too deaf to cope with the business on his own, agreed at last, reluctantly, to give it up. He went to work once more in the hated factories, and mom found herself at home again. But her children were beginning to make little trial flights from the nest. One son was already married and embarked on a many years' nomadic pursuit of higher education. And the rest of us were beginning to twitch our feathers too. Chaia Waisman entered semi-retirement to be confronted by the prospect of soon being left utterly alone with her new leisure.

When did you start making dolls in earnest?
> What, did you forget the polio?

The last great polio epidemic, just before the discovery of the Salk vaccine, hit Winnipeg and the far North in 1950. The new Princess Elizabeth Hospital had opened not long before. My sister had designed the lab and was chief medical technologist of the isolation and chronic illness cluster of hospitals. During the epidemic she would come home with tales of even Inuit being flown in paralysed, and of children, children filling the wards. Mother proceeded to nag my big sister to get her taken on as a volunteer ward aid at the hospitals. She, who had always claimed that she could never raise her heavy head from the pillow until the sun dragged it up on his climb, now rushed off with my sister early in the mornings. "For four months they had to chase me out of the hospital." She immersed herself, cleaning the patients, reading to them, telling them stories, playing with them, eating her lunch with them, championing them, scolding nurses where necessary, bearding even the medical staff over any breach of care of her charges. "Mama, come back!" the children would call to her when she passed along the corridors. Of their suffering, "It hurted me," she explains. "I felt good when I helped." Long after she came down with the infection which sent her into hospital as a patient, and ended her career on the wards, she was still receiving letters from her little ex-patients.

The dolls began to flow. I remember helping to carry bags and boxes full of them to the hospitals whenever I happened to be handy and she had a batch ready to be taken off to the wards. I didn't take too much note, though, being at that time very much otherwise preoccupied, in that most egocentric age of all, my phenomenally extended late adolescence. But a long while later, I was reminded of what she must have been like on those wards, when a well known Winnipeg pediatrician, himself an ex polio victim, who had been one of the young doctors on duty on those wards, and who had not seen my mother for years, refused to bill a visiting little patient when he heard that this was Mrs. Waisman's granddaughter.

> *And then all of a sudden, in one week, five of my children went away, my whole family. Suddenly my house was still, my town become a hamlet.*
> Overhearing, I realize the fifth child was Harry's Esther. But the rest?
> > *Mama, I heard you tell that lady we all went away in the same week. We never left home all in the same week!*
> > *You did. You've forgotten. I can't forget.*

I am forced to remember. She is right, of course. That's how it happened to her. She had always known that at the other end of the turbulent journey which would, at last, hopefully, allow them "to bring their children to a shore," of which she so longingly spoke, there lurked the dreaded transformation of her metaphor, at which point, as she so often warned us, bracing herself verbally, we would insist on "flying from the nest," as she herself had so regretfully done. Now Marjm was going East for graduate work; Harry and Esther were taking yet another trailer south to yet another university for work on yet another degree; Mo was graduating and thinking of work or further study down East too, and I, with a novel begun, was about to take the artist's initiation rites of my day, and make my queasy way across the ocean to steep myself in Yurrup and Cultsha. Mama was about to be beached in an empty nest. Yes, I must grant the reality of the shock of our nearly simultaneous departure. For me too the events of that time are curiously foreshortened, with a kind of emotional simultaneity. But in fairness she must admit that we have proved ourselves to this day to be very much a family of round-trippers, an ageing lot of perpetual fledglings of the spirit, quick to call for help or fly home for comfort, whole families of us still rocking that nest over the perilous waves of the mixed metaphor of existence.

I am almost ready to leave, but who can believe it? I am vaguely aware that mama is taking it all far too seriously. She seems to fear that I, in particular, will be lost to them, since I have earned only a one-way ticket, and am going all the way to England. Her own experience tells her that when you take that long journey overseas, you do not return, and though I try to reassure her I have no intention of staying away forever, she fears what she fears. But she will not try to stop me.

I want to tell you something. Mama leads me into their bedroom. She closes the door mysteriously. She takes my hand and presses it to her belly. Her face is flushed, with a curious, half smiling, enquiring expression. *Feel?*
I feel.
> *Is something the matter?* I ask stupidly.
> *Can't you feel it? Here, I'll lie down.* She lies back on the old,

much-patched pink tick cover, still smiling her slightly embarrassed smile.

> *Put your ear down; here, listen.*

I press my ear against her big, elastic tum, listen blankly to
amiable gurgles.

> *Well?* mama laughs at my dullness. *Do you need I should put a
finger in your mouth? Can't you hear the heartbeat?*

Miraculously she is a pregnant young woman again, her eyes
as dream-infested by the future as our own. She is glad that her
grown children are not fiercely embarrassed, as she had
feared we might be. Insofar as we pay much attention, poised
as we are to take off at last in search of LIFE, we allow, with
magnanimity, that it might even be good for her to have something to occupy her during our absence.

For me she has packed the enormous old steamer trunk with
linen and bedding and tinned goods and cooking utensils and
even the basic ingredients for my favourite soup, two pounds
of split peas in a brown paper bag which will later split, and
pinkl pinkl pinkl all over the front hallway of the Settlement as
I make my debut in East London, in full view of the entire
incredulous staff and half the kids of the agency, to whom I am
bringing the polish and sophistication and glamour that
comes, at this time, with being almost-a-Yank, in accent anyway. The trunk is so heavy I have had to unpack it publicly,
because the elderly little ex-seaman caretaker can't carry it up
the stairs for fear of "ruining himself" ("all over again," as one
of the club cleaners is to inform me at a later date. She has
discovered his prior ruination at firsthand in the course of
trying to earn an honest extra shilling to pass on to her part-
time "man," who has a wife and family to support). For
encore, on my arrival, I have two huge battered tin suitcases
covered with mysterious markings, which mom has pur-

chased from our "displaced person" neighbours for my trip.

When mama returns from seeing her doctor, a few days after the revelation of her pregnancy, she says only, with a small sideways inclination of the head, *He laughed at me,* and she laughs, a little wryly, at herself.
For an instant I perceive her world from within. Comprehension threatens. I can't cope right now so I pack it away, hastily. "This is going to mean something to me someday, when I have time to think about it." I actually formulate the thought.

For the next two years I was to write passionate letters home in kitchen Yiddish, proclaiming my need for growth, describing my search for adventure and understanding, performing all the post-though-not-quite-past adolescent verbal fandangoes inspired by the young writer's first trip abroad, with her head, as often as her novel, tucked underneath her arm. And yet I don't know what, in all my wanderings, has haunted me more persistently than that memory of my mother's wry little shrug, which has burst, time and again, pinkl pinkl pinkl into my consciousness. There was a period when I was tempted to blow up the pathos of this memory. But from this impulse to fondle and reduce to bathos the reality of the moment she herself has liberated me over the years. Surrounded by her dolls I know she doesn't need the condescension of my pity. When we left she settled down to making and giving up the gift of her babies to the world in earnest.

But mama, why do you make them?
> *Why do you ask questions?*
> *You think maybe it's the same thing?*

Mama shrugs. If she has bothered me occasionally by kicking at her bucket, I certainly have reciprocated with this persistent banging on her kettle, as the Yiddish expression would have it. We continue at cross purposes, though we really do our best to co-operate.

Home for a visit, I have no sooner settled into the house when mama announces, *I want you to telephone the Medical College and tell them I want to donate my body.*
No amount of teasing, of hailing her the premature corpse of the century, of putting it off till later, will work this time. So I telephone the Dept. of Pathology at the University of Manitoba, and ask for the man in charge of donated bodies. The Pathologist listens quietly while I explain that my mother wants to arrange for her future. Finally, to my astonishment, he remarks, *That wouldn't be Mrs. Waisman of Burrows Ave., would it?*

I had arrived home from an extended work-stay in Rome, some years before, with a magpie collection of curios. Among them, carefully wrapped in a canvas tote sac, were several parts of a human skull and some plain but very ancient shards of pottery. My landlords in the Italian capital had been excavating, and uncovered these remains. They had reported to the Dept. of Antiquities, and their find had been duly examined, and judged more than two thousand years old, but probably belonging to a servant and therefore not very valuable in a country which still has antique aristocracy and very fancy potsherds to dig up. So my friends had let me have the remains, which I toted home, reasoning that in democratic young Manitoba even plebeian bones and shards of a certain age would have some glamour.

I left these souvenirs behind when I set out once again to rummage in the world. Mama decided that objects which might be of incalculable educational value should not be left mouldering in a canvas bag, and figuring that old bones would be of most interest in a medical school, she had called up the college. The pathologist, who had been sufficiently intrigued to come out to examine her treasures, and had stayed to have tea and a chat, did not forget.

Unbeknown to me, when I picked up that phone, the stage had already been set for the realization of Chaika Waisman's great dream of post-mortem romance. But when has that course ever run smooth?

The simple form in which the next-of-kin waives claim to the body has arrived. I fill it in and bring it to my father to sign. Here the great conflict begins. Curiously enough, though you have the right to determine who shall inherit your goods after your death, that right does not extend to the post-mortem disposition of your body. Though he claims he is not religious, my father has a strong sense of tradition, and Hebrews do not mutilate or burn their corpses.

Mother is outraged. *It's my body! I can do what I want with my body!*

Rocking on heel and sole, smiling beatifically, daddy qualifies carefully. *You can do what you want, but I'm not signing any paper.*

The children will sign.

They can if they want to. As he moves off, the rasping purr of his song has already risen in his throat. Unspoken is the knowledge between them that the children are now usually far away.

He'll sign, she vows darkly. *He'll sign.*

Daddy is once again on his ceaseless round of the house, his sandpaper voice grating forth one of the familiar songs of his youth.

Doesn't even get the lyrics right, she mutters. *Oh he'll sign by me. I'll get him to sign all right.*

There is nothing morbid in mother's attitude to death. She is matter-of-fact. Death, at a certain point, appears on the near side of one's life and she simply wants, in this as in most things, to make it serve the living. It is in pursuit of this ideal that she pioneers cadaver lib so strenuously.

Has dad signed yet? has become a form of family greeting.Mom invariably brings the subject up when we meet, appealing to her children, her grievance simmering, her indignation unabated. And dad, though progressively more deaf, remains ever sensitive to that fiery glance. Catching it, he pauses an instant to check inward with widened eyes; then, reassured of his own innocence, he gets himself nimbly out of range, sending out, nevertheless, from a safe distance, his familiar splinters of song in token of his steadfast heart and conscience clear.

Her references to death have the quality, not of an obsession, but of a recurring theme in a large composition, a theme which provides part of the balance of the whole, a necessary theme. I must confess that some of the funniest, most memorable conversations I've had with my mom in these later years have centred on the subject of her death. Once, for some reason, Marjm, mama and I got onto the subject of "suttee," the East Indian custom in which the wife was expected to throw herself on her husband's funeral pyre.

Would you do it for me, Peisy? mom calls out to dad, who has wandered within earshot. *Will you throw yourself on the fire after me, like an Indian Prince?*
My father laughs, and skips with agility out of range of the smouldering coals of the old controversy.
Well, mama shrugs, *so throw in a few potatoes.*
Into the ensuing laughter, *Be like this when the time comes,* she says suddenly. *When it happens, laugh. Don't cry.*

And on another occasion:

You'll bury my scissors and my thimble with me, she instructs.
> *But you want to be cremated.*
> *With my ashes, then. I'll take them to the grave.*

> *Okay, when you pop off at a hundred and twenty-one we'll bury them with you.*
> *Don't be foolish.* She is all scorn. *Who needs a hundred and twenty-one?* She shudders at the idea, her skin, somewhat less rosy than it was only yesterday, but only just beginning to show trace of wrinkle, is genuinely repelled. *Let your father have his hundred and twenty-one years. I don't want them.* She broods a moment. *But who'll take care of him?*
Mama sighs and turns to her sewing. Turn and turn again, and thread and cut and patch and mend and make and learn, finally, to understand that you may not be allowed to tuck in neatly all the ends of your life.

───────────

Nowadays she no longer has to deliver her doll shipments herself. A phone call brings a social worker. I don't know whether she ever bothers to count the number of creatures in any particular shipment; certainly, she has kept no overall tally. I do remember one satisfied numerical account I received though. She and dad had been in Miami again, looking after their orphaned grandson.

A couple of the kids' old friends came over to see us. They do voluntary work down there with the underprivileged children. They were telling me that for Christmas they had to have presents for forty-eight children. So I said 'All right,' and in less than two weeks I had made them forty-eight dolls. Every single child in the class had a doll for Christmas.
> *How long does it take you to make a doll?*
> *Oh about two hours.*

Even during those days when the five-room bungalow on Burrows Ave. contained not only the six of us, but a variety of roomers, sometimes whole families of them, there were periods when both the electric range in the kitchen and the big black wood stove in the cellar were hot with the activity of my mother and other women preparing for a banquet at the Yiddish school or the Free Loan Society. As soon as they gave up the shop, mom became a volunteer worker with the Golden Age Club, in which she eventually graduated to member. That her standards of social responsibility continue to be exacting, my sister was in no uncertain way reminded not too long ago.

It must be understood that my sister, Marjm Hannah, is herself a formidable lady. She has to be, to have survived with intact identity not only that first gouging attack on the child by the teacher who announced, "Marjm? That's no name. I'll call you 'Mary,'" from which she managed to salvage "Miriam," but all the subsequent humiliations and frustrated hopes, the early crude and later more subtle attacks on the sense of worth of one who bled internally, but nevertheless refused to accept that being immigrant, female, poor and a Jew are handicaps. As a mother of two, and even at the time when she had a full-time job in biochemical research at a post-doctoral level, she could still manage to keep a spotless home, be active in the Home and School association, help run a science club at the school, do abstracts for a scientific journal in order to keep abreast of her field, work for the perpetuation of Yiddish education, and withal manage to relax at a concert sometimes, go dancing sometimes, sometimes entertain friends. Her home is the centre of our latter-day periodic family outbreaks of celebration: weddings, anniversaries, Bar Mitzvah, and so on, for which people from several continents have gathered. There are always guests staying with her; when I see her she is always busy, always doing, always with a list of chores and imperatives as long as her arm. When I return from a visit with her I can only bring myself to face the chaos toward which my surroundings perpetually tend by reminding myself sternly that after all, inadequacy too is a way of life. One of the hardest facts I ever had to learn to accept in late childhood was that my big sister could ever possibly be wrong about anything. "My big sister said so," was my final seal to any argument, even as far on as my high school years. And yet, it was this same big sister who, still reeling, called me one day long-distance to repeat a conversation she'd just had with our Chaika.

> Everyone else asleep, mom and her eldest settle in for the traditional first-night-of-the-visit-all-night-chat which characterizes visits among us. My sister, urged by mom, details her activities, describes her long, crowded days that spill over into late evenings and too short, exhausted nights, and mom listens, tsk tsking over the strains, advising against the excesses, giggling over the anecdotes, worrying about the tiredness, admonishing, sympathizing, encouraging.
> Finally, into the drained, companionable pause with which they greet the dawn, mama enquires gently, *And what are you doing for the community?*

I don't believe my sister and I ever actually set out to collect the dolls. It was simply a process of spontaneous accumulation at first. They were such fun to look at.

> *Can I have this one, ma?*
> > *All right. That's her husband. Take the pair.*
> > *And these? Oh, and this couple?*
> > *All right. Take.*
> > *What about him? And her? How can I leave these? Look at that face!*
> > *Take. Take. I'll make more.*

In a world where people define themselves and evaluate each other according to what they have, and what they can get, it is a change to find someone who seems to define herself by what she can make and what she can give. The onus is then on the taker to learn to cope with her greed.

Even the humblest disciple of and assistant to nature can make suggestions and hope by the magical logic of her own creation to influence, if only imperceptibly, the bias of reality. Chaika Waisman would like to banish loneliness from the earth. All her dolls have partners, except for the fluffy ones which are meant to partner very small children. Though often the partners are husband and wife, they by no means have to be. Sisters, friends, twins, as long as "everybody has somebody," she is content, and I believe hopes that nature too will take the hint and act toward the greater general contentment. Not infrequently she used to find in my home that some of her couples had got separated. "Where's her husband?" she'd say, turning to me. "We'll have to find her a mate." Sometimes I couldn't remember which one had been the original mate, though I am more careful now, more hesitant to play the part of careless fate in sundering the delicate bonds of creation. Mama can usually remember who belongs to whom, as they are often actually conceived as a pair, with simultaneously created interrelating biographies. But even if she can't remember offhand which two she'd paired originally, she doesn't pause to mourn, but straightway selects mates that "could go together." She is not, I might add, as easygoing about re-coupling in her own life. Others may, or even should, if widowed, eventually re-marry, to defeat that destructive loneliness, but not Clara Waisman. Her "enslavement" is for keeps. "A fine fool I'd look." She nods toward dad. "He can, though, probably will." She chuckles wickedly, "old fool."

Her sexual attitudes are similarly flexible toward others, personally stern. Children and animals have the blessing of open innocence. On a small boy doll I have occasionally noted a healthy thread penis a-dangle. Under the tail of a small fur creature I have often found a meticulously created little red arsehole. But at a certain age adults zipper up, and their sex lives, sometimes clearly indicated in the biographical anecdotes with which she accompanies the dolls, may be gleaned perhaps only by a very careful reading of the dolls themselves.

He's one of those French types you hear about, mama murmurs, holding up a particularly elegant fellow with a natty tam, an impressively coiffed beard and moustache, slender, long arms and legs, impeccable tailoring. *He looks after himself and dresses just-so, and he likes to run after women. His wife,* mama sighs, *she dresses smartly, does her best. What can she do?*

They say there are no new plots in the world. What is fascinating is to see in what terms every imaginative human being rediscovers and reinterprets the existent realities and shibboleths, what cultural influences are reflected in and reflect for her most validly her own perceptions, what images and metaphors appear to the artist to be analogous to her own reality. How often, for instance, mama makes clown dolls, "because the children love them." And she describes, with face aglow, the circuses and travelling zoos of her childhood.

The clowns, always with a big belly hanging in front, and the girls on horseback, in their beautiful costumes, doing tricks.

But how often her clown dolls have a small, stylized thread of tear below one eye.

> *What's that, mama?*
> *> It's a tear.*
> *> Why's he crying?*
> *> Well, you know, that's life. 'Laugh, clown laugh.' His heart could be breaking.*
> *> Do you want children to see him like that?*
> *> Children don't cry too? See how nicely he's dressed? They can play with him.*

The dolls in this sense too, far from being an escape from reality,

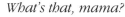

are a learning to live, "to play" with it, as is most childhood play and its tools.

Many of the dolls are indissolubly linked together in my mind by the vignettes with which she has opened up past and future and established indelibly the quality of their being or the tone of their relationship. I watched her make one little couple at my kitchen table. She worked on both simultaneously, making, alternately, a bit of one and a bit of the other, so that they actually grew into being together, as some folktales would have couples on earth predestined for each other in heaven. As with the single doll one part suggests another, the form, feel, quality, shape the other should take, so too when she is creating two together, the parts grope their way to their own interrelated whole. As simple as possible in construction, each is about a foot long; each is made of a bit of old panty-hose, the male navy blue, the female grey mauve stuffed with dark material. Some of the basic form of each is achieved by knotting. For instance each of the husband's wrists is a knot in the material, from which the spatular toe-end of a foot of the panty-hose expresses "hand."

Well! Mama sounds slightly surprised. She pats the little doll's round belly, to which she has added a white stitched belly button to go with the two white nipples above. *She's pregnant!* Now she picks up the young man. *He's an English type of young fellow. See his big teeth?* His teeth, two prominent white double stitches, buck out above the orange threaded lips. *But he looks too young to take care of a pregnant wife,* mama muses. She brightens. *We'll give him whiskers.* And soon after, *There!* Mama triumphant, has added a formidable pair of brown-gold winged moustaches. *Now he's more mature for his responsibilities.*

She has co-ordinated the free flow of her ideas to achieve the imagination's logical conclusions.

Because she gets bored with doing the same thing, she will sometimes announce, "I'm tired of making dolls. I'll make something else for a change." This is when the cutwork tablecloths begin to emerge, the highly individual embroidery pictures, in which she selects a pre-stamped picture, of the kind used for gros-point stitching, and proceeds to improvise on it her own stitches and pattern variations and colours, so that the end result has often a remarkable effect of brush work and depths of unsuspected perspective and character. Unpacking of the new creations has been a highlight of parental visits over the years, as has the stripping of walls and chairs and couches of the old homestead when we visit.

Take, take, she shrugs. *So I'll have to make more.* She tries to look appropriately victimized, but her sigh has turned itself inside out and emerges a small chuckle.

How to describe the quality of their journeys and arrivals? It could never possibly be a question of simply pack bags and away. Even the sturdiest of suitcases somehow lose their shape in mother's hands, have to be roped, strapped, webbed in with patiently created multiple coloured-rag webbing. And no matter how many suitcases they accumulate there are never enough. Always there is a most extraordinary assortment of parcels and packages and shopping bags stuffed beyond recognition, achieving indefinable shapes, tied with multicoloured bits of knotted string and rope and ribbons and sewn into sacs created from variegated scraps of cloth, all bumpy and lumpy and mysterious. Always there are several which mom simply has to carry in person. Sometimes they are almost as heavy as she, cunningly layered, with the strudl on top to offer the customs man so he won't look underneath and find the corned beef, about which customs officials are reputed to be inexplicably snarky. And on the return, plants. Why would customs officials confiscate your plants if you didn't hide them?

Look, mama, plants carry diseases sometimes. They don't want you to contaminate our own plant life.
> *I only bring clean ones. We don't even see this kind in Canada.*
> *I'm warning you, mama. They'll put you in jail.*
> *So I'll sit.*

We await border crossings with tremulous misgiving, but mama always saunters through. If she were going to worry about the nit-picking of fussy officialdom she'd never manage to complete these journeys and bring husband, luggage and livestock through intact. Of course there's livestock too. Who can afford the kennel charges for your animals over visits which sometimes last for months? It's far cheaper to bring the current menagerie along with you. When we grown children had all moved elsewhere mom could not bear being alone in the house without "living things to talk to."

She casts a meaningful glance at dad.
All he does is read, read the Yiddish paper all day. And you think he reads only important things, what's going on in the world? Mama snorts. All the advice the doctors give somebody else he reads, so every time I turn around he's pushing another plate away, 'I don't eat this, it's no good for me,' though it's been good enough for eighty years. And he loves the letters from all the gossips and the crazy old men who think their wives are poisoning them. He believes everything. It's in the paper, it must be so. You should see sometimes the way he looks at me when I give him a cup of tea. 'Did you boil the water? You didn't boil the water, I didn't hear the water boil!' Since when has he even been able to hear water boiling? And he stands and watches me and peers into the kettle. Sixty years later I'm going to poison him and run off with my young sweetheart. That's our conversation, did I boil the water. Otherwise all day his head's in the paper.

And so they arrive with birdcages and a whole series of budgies, variously named according to colour and fancy, "Honey Cake," "Lemon Pie," "Lettuce." And canaries. And cats criss-crossing the continent by air. And dogs. My own boxer Big Julie, whom she raised when I was not allowed to keep him in my Montreal apartment, and whom she subsequently baby-sat at various intervals during his eleven years, was an enviably travelled animal, and was once delivered before the eyes of all Burrows Ave., seated regal in solitary splendour on the back seat of the airport limousine, because he'd got on the wrong plane in Miami. "Showed those neighbours who snubbed us because we were merely tailoring workers, when we first moved in, forty years ago, that where true worth is recognized, even the dogs of mere tailors can rise beyond the dreams of fools."

Once they baby-sat my brother's greyhound Honey, the animal through whom I finally understood why the ancients sometimes regarded beauty and grace as supreme virtues in themselves, and brought Honey as well as the splendid ginger cat "Big Julius Too," who straightway on arrival required emergency surgery on a blocked urinary tract. Which of the warblers sang along that time? Or do I confuse the times? The chaos of those arrivals! First the anxious waiting around, straining to catch sight of diminutive forms at the head of stairs, because mom gets dizzy on escalators, worrying whether dad has let them put him in a wheelchair this time, for the long walk, an expedient he has strenuously fought off for years, preferring his "glycerine" pills to the indignity of public invalidism. What a relief, after the waiting, when we know that they actually must have arrived though we haven't caught sight of them yet, because somebody's spotted the "funniest baggage in the airport." And then, briefly, contact, and dad promptly disappearing to hunt up toilet or ticket counter, and everybody taking off in different directions in search, connections missed, animal cages arriving and dogs dragging us out of buildings to empty their steaming bladders invariably under the noses of grim-faced guards.

What will it be next time, birds, turtles, dogs, cats, goldfish? Anything living, just so "it should be gay in the house."

> From the bedroom a scuffle and a yelp as dad tries to slip out and leave the pup to his training paper. Who won this time? Daddy, apparently. Tranquil, he appears, not, for once, in futile chase. *She wants a dog so let her have a dog.* He sighs, shrugs, tolerant or resigned, at eighty-one. He glances at her, his expression wary, implying that it might have been something worse. From the bedroom sounds of the dog chaotically teething on everything in sight. For mom it will be shredded bedlinen again tonight, and she'll say wonderingly, *Have you ever seen such a dog?*

> Thousands of times, mama, in this very house, all my life.

> *I've never seen such a dog,* she affirms cheerfully. *But maybe he'll grow into a person yet.*

My father always hopes, each time they set out on their nomadic round, that this time mother will somehow be persuaded to stay on longer in Miami. "I'm cold everywhere else," he explains to each of us in turn. "But I can't," says mama. "I can't stand the clammy heat down there. It doesn't let you breathe." One of the few characteristics she shares with her seventy-year-old kid sister Sonia is a passion for the winters of Winnipeg, for the subtle stages of the settling in of snow, its varied boot music, the northern blues, softly groaning underfoot, then squeaking and grunting our sole melodies, and finally, intimate companion of deep winter, barking at every heel. They love the glittering dry jewelled needles stabbing their pipes as they breathe. "I can't stand anything around my neck," says mama defiantly, refusing to button her coat collar, and exposing the bronchitis-prone chest to the forty-degrees-below-Fahrenheit weather. "Ah, ah!" she cries, "Air! Air!" Beside her, sunk, barely visible in his layer-on-layer of combinations and sweaters and massive fur hat and fur-lined overcoat, my father shudders.

Have they ever, though so closely linked, in all their years together taken a journey which has meant the same to them both? Even that first long voyage, the Odyssey, or perhaps the Iliad might be more precise, of my father's young manhood, when he undertook to escort and deliver his unlettered sister and her four small children to the husband waiting somewhat less than eagerly in Canada, was most reluctantly agreed to by my mother, as a duty and a favour to a helpless sister-in-law. She never wanted to leave her own family. Her reception in Canada at the hands of her brother-in-law was a shocking contrast to the family life she had known.

> *'Take me home,' I begged your father. He wouldn't. 'So send me home, you can stay. Let me go,' I implored him. 'I'll even leave you the children, anything, only let me go home!'* Mama sighs, shrugs. *Stub-born. 'Well then, at least take me to my kin in Winnipeg.'*
> In some corner of her being she has never ceased to be homesick.

What had my father to be homesick about? Orphaned at eight he had been thrust from dreams of scholarship and cantorial pre-eminence, to experience a more brutish existence. His mother's sister had been married to a skilled tailor, a "wealthy" man. One day someone came running to tell her that her husband was being beaten by neighbours in an argument over pride of place in the synagogue. A man's social position was indicated by where he sat in the synagogue and in those backward hamlets fine social distinctions were often made in summary fashion. Dad's aunt seized a stave and rushed to her husband's assistance. She was intercepted by the neighbour, the stave was wrested from her, and she was beaten so badly that within three weeks she died. My dad was apprenticed at nine to his now re-married uncle. The offending neighbour told him, "Your uncle has nothing to complain about. He should thank me; I enabled him to get himself a brand new young wife."

My uncle had it in for me. When I was apprenticed to him he always threw it up to me that when my father was alive I had once said that uncle had nothing to be proud of. Could he even read a page of Holy Writ? I don't even remember saying it. I was five years old!

Within a few years my father had provided dowries for and married off two elder sisters. He had purchased a cow too, for his mother, and helped provide the basic sustenance which kept her and his two crippled brothers alive. At twelve he took advantage of the dispensation which allows for an earlier entry into man's estate for orphans, and arranged and carried through his own Bar Mitzvah. When his cousin deliberately muffed the opportunity to become a shoe salesman in a larger town, in order to force his father to teach him tailoring, because his girl-friend's family were emigrating to South America and she had told the boy that craftsmen, not salesmen were needed there, the uncle's chagrin was great. Salesmen in his world were a cut above people who worked with their hands. The boy did not learn as quickly as he might have and his father beat him mercilessly. Consequently, when dad's year was up he refused to return to work for his uncle until he had extracted a promise that he would stop brutalizing his own son.

How my dad still exults over each obstacle overcome, each triumph of survival which he managed to engineer for his two women and five little children during the months of wandering across Europe toward the new world.

Once we were over the border I was surrounded immediately by upturned faces. Daddy raises his face ceilingward, flowers his lips outward, *'FOOD!' my sister and her four children cry out to me. 'FOOD!' your mother holding the child in her arms. Straightway I went into the town. Polish is similar to Russian and I could recognize some signs. I entered a tailor's shop and found he was a Jew. So I said, 'Do you have work for me?'*
'What Jew,' he said, 'seeks work on a Friday?'
'I do,' said I. 'We've just crossed the border. I must eat.'
'You'll have work here,' he said.
'I have a wife and child,' I said. 'Do you know of a place we could sleep?'
'I know a place,' he said, and led me next door, where the shoichet's wife made business. 'Give him a room,' he said to her, 'and I will supply him with a bed and a cushion.'
She agreed.
'Perhaps you need a few mark?' he asked me.
'If you have God in your heart!' I cried. 'They stripped us clean at the border.'
He put his hand in his pocket and handed me two thousand mark. Two thousand mark! To me it was as though an angel had appeared and flung it down from the heavens. When he had gone I said to the woman, 'I have a sister with four children.'
'Bring them here,' she said.
I returned where I had left them waiting. 'Sit,' I said. 'We'll eat now.' There on the green grass of that place I sat them down and I brought out the two herring and the big round bread I had bought.' His hands and eyes sketch simultaneously the size of the bread and the size of the astonished eyes of his dependants, and my father laughs, on his face the expression which his seven-year-old granddaughter brings her friends to

see. 'My zedah laughs just like a baby!'

When they had eaten their fill I said, 'Come with me now, I've found a place for you.' That woman, the shoichet's wife had a big table, where people came to play billiards during the day. At night she turned it into a bed for my sister and her family. This settled, I gave my sister a few mark and my wife a few mark, and I said to them, 'Now go, buy what you need.'

My father chuckles and rocks on the edge of the hospital bed; his legs, which do not reach the floor, sketch out nevertheless the familiar stamping movement that has marked all his angers and his triumphs, which seems to me the echo of some primeval rearing gesture of the male. At 84 he is in hospital to check signs of incipient heart failure. Before entrusting me once again with this fragment of his saga, he has informed me, with a little boy's laughter, that this morning the nurse had waked him by tickling his toes.

Over the years, across the barriers of his deafness and of a language he never had time to learn properly, and friendships he never had the opportunity to learn to make, these stories have become my father's presentation of himself to a world which seldom spares him an ear. But he rehearses anyway, for to my father, though often disappointed, cut-off, turned-in, defeat is not a relevant concept. In his old age he pursues through the lived terrain of his life, the high mystery of his existence. Whether speaking in the natural fluency of his mother tongue, Yiddish, or stumbling gamely through his English, he searches out analogies, recognizes correspondences, traces through the myriad confusing shapes of his past a meaningful shapeliness. He perceives his life with the selectivity of an artist, recreating it mentally as an art work, or an article of religious faith. Like any artist or visionary he will gladly share it with you. If he catches your eye my father will quickly offer you that portion of the adventure of his life, purged of inessentials, on which he has been currently musing. It is a modest story, but haunted as are all human lives by strange and evocative resonances. And it reveals irrefutably that he has been a faithful link in an honourable chain of being. Ceaselessly he navigates the conquered territories of his own narrowing lifestream, eager at any time to take you along to marvel with him at the lifescape of a man's existence, a lifescape cleanly outlined by significant details so formalized that they resemble the scenes of true myth, my father's life safe now from misinterpretation or attack, protected in its final shape by the very hardening of the arteries through which his lifestream flows.

Unfortunately, among the inessentials expunged almost entirely from my father's story of his life, is the part my mother played.

> *Do you hear that? HE went and HE did and HE said and HE worked and HE helped and HE saved. And what of me? There was never a moment when I wasn't there, slaving by his side, working stitch by seam along with him from the moment of our marriage. During all those very months when HE did this and HE did that, when we wandered from place to place, not only did I have to look after his sister, poor thing thrust out of her little hamlet into the world she was so bewildered, she couldn't help herself from one minute to the next, but I had to see to all the children, and even so I took in sewing, everywhere we went. My life has passed, stitch for stitch together with his. When does a tailor sew for naught? When he forgets to knot his thread. When I hear your father talk and I remind him that I too was there, all the time, working beside him, he says 'So you helped me out a little bit sometimes.' Fifty-seven years and as far as he remembers I need never once have knotted my thread.*

If my father's song of his life is recognizably the ancient, proud, blinkered chauvinism of the male, my mother's cry of protest at being edited-out rings a truly modern note of female exasperation. When I told her how one of her granddaughters had punched out a little boy who had pulled her chair out from under her at the children's synagogue, she remarked, "He's always liked her, even as far back as kindergarten he used to help her put her boots on. But Vivy's hot tempered, like her grandmother."

And when I pursued it, "But mama, in synagogue? on Yom Kippur?" she replied serenely, "Nobody's going to spit in her kasha."

I believe that I owe whatever balance I managed to achieve in spite of the rigours of my public school years, to my mother's recognition of my right to protest. Regularly, I would get sent home and told not to come back until my mother had come to see the principal. Mama would put down her sewing, and even though I was shouting after her, "Don't go! Make them come to you!" she would set out. On her return, I could gather little from her sparse replies to my furious questions other than that all of my teachers had appeared, each to recite her separate tale of my wickedness. "Ganging up" as usual, beneath my snorting contempt.

So what happened?
> *So I begged them, whatever they do to discipline you, not to send you away from the school I shouldn't know where you are and you should run around in the streets and meet all kinds of bad. The same as I beg them not to do with Harry every time they call me.*
Suddenly, mama is smiling, and the one relevant piece of information which has got through to her during all the earnest hectoring of her school visit emerges. *They say you could be a leader if you wanted to.*

Years later I told her how grateful I was that she and my dad had never borne down on me for my apparently delinquent behaviour at school. "I could see you were unhappy," she replied.

To this day, even in her illness, mama still brings treasure. Not only toys and dolls and pictures and hangings and embroidery and cutwork emerge from those strange, gypsy bundles. Unsolicited, she still makes nearly all my clothes, and a great deal of my sister's wardrobe, too, as well as a constant flow of costumes for the grandchildren.

evening gowns	hats	rag rugs
redingotes	handbags	toilet-roll covers
silk-tie creations	capes	placemats
bedspreads	scarves	tablecloths
fancy cushions	ties	nightgowns
highly original quilts	necklaces	pillowslips
colourful throws	blouses	blankets
skirts	mobiles	drapes
dresses	muffs	curtains
dressing gowns	poufs	underwear
coats	shawls	

AND MORE, including the inevitable "ehpehs," "I don't know what it is, maybe you could use it for fancy." For a while she was crocheting circular rag potholders, which sometimes grew big enough to be used as placemats, and sometimes developed an oceanic, wavy flair. These she then proceeded to put under my tablelamps and other whatnots "for fancy," so that my whatnots and lamps developed interesting skew stances which sometimes make my guests a little nervous. Then suddenly her potholders began to grow faces, huge ears, hats, curious appendages, and another kind of doll was born—or mask reborn. She may have been briefly tired of making dolls, but once rested, the profound need emerged in her again, to confer identity, reality, life. Of late her potholders and egg and tea cosies have been exploring ornithological possibilities, and whole new strains of brilliant birds-as-they-might-be have come to roost among us, in all their kooky cockiness.

As a dressmaker, she has over the years displayed an uncanny pre-science in guessing the current state of her daughters' figures. For years she brought clothes she'd made for us sight unseen, from the most elaborately fanciful in style, to suit my sister's taste for high fashion, to the simpler lines she finally had reluctantly to adopt to suit my blunter mode. Always the clothes fit. Well, not quite always; sometimes, she allowed, her mind must have wandered, and we were made uneasily aware that she actually is ageing. But it's hard to tell with her.

> *I guess they're a bit too big, mom,* I say almost apologetically, as I stand holding up around me a massive pair of new shorts.
> *Oh,* she replies calmly, *I must be losing my cut. Of course you haven't gained as much weight as I thought.*
> And I wonder uneasily how far she has lost her cut and how far and just how absent-mindedly she has projected my current trend, for my own edification.

Our elders often find it convenient to assume, when confronted with the vigorous self-assertiveness of climbing youth and peaking middle age, a certain ingenuousness which I have occasionally had cause to query. Mind you we bring it on ourselves. Once I had become aware that the dolls were speaking to me, and was becoming more and more obsessed by the suggestive mystery of them, I got into the habit, as I have already indicated, of shamelessly wheedling her creations from her, cadging and cajoling and even, on occasion, whining that she was giving my big sister more dolls than she was giving me. I am not above manipulating maternal guilt a bit, in a good cause. She was so obviously distressed to be accused of favouring one child over another, and it worked so well that I carried it on for years. And then once, well satisfied with my loot, I was startled to catch her glance, and to recognize something like pity in her eyes. I realized then that I must have long since ceased to work effective blackmail on maternal guilt, and that she responded now as required out of wry tolerance for my own needs.

> *Do you know what this couple are saying?* I ask hopefully, trying out a new formula.
> > *What should they say?*
> > *Like, for instance, why did you make them in particular?*
> > *Don't you like them? Look how nice I made her feet in the long fancy boots they wear to dance. And her partner in his elegant clothes that fit like a glove. Aren't they beautiful? Just like real Spanish dancers!*

Just like, though no point-by-point stylized reproduction this, of the kind that you bring back for the children from your trips abroad. Through some uncanny process of observation she has reproduced the very feel of these people. I recognize these dancers. I've seen them in Paris and in London and on the concert stage in Canada too. And the woman is indeed usually somewhat plumper than the man, and sometimes even taller. Mom's lady is arresting in her black lace over deep green costume billowing seductively from around the detergent bottle which is her base. Her mantilla falls in graceful folds from her peaked hat, and her long neck is rich in dark metallic stuff. On her white cotton face are not one but two of mother's grace notes, the "beauty spots" I have elsewhere noted. But it is the expression on this face which I recognize anew each time I look at her. The large, black stitched eyes have blue pupils which are just the faintest bit cockeyed, and together with the slightly smiling mouth express just that marvelous combination of surprise, triumph and self-satisfaction which I have seen on the faces of lady Spanish dancers and belly dancers too, when they feel they are really "doing it." And her partner, her sinewy heel-stomper in his blue on blue skintight brocade, with his long, slender legs and intricate pointed shoes, all man for all he's smaller and thinner than she, on his face the expression of confident mastery of one who knows that aficionados watching breathlessly will turn with ferocity on the dumb little Canadian broad who is thoughtless enough to absent-mindedly strike a match in the dark Parisian night club during his performance. And that rightly apologetic broad, caught once again profaning a temple of art, knows she never will be sure that she will not, sometime, inadvertently do it yet once again.

For alas, I never was one of those special little girls I used to read about with such passionate envy, those star-touched moppets with the natural, spontaneous, untutored gift of unerring response to TRUE BEAUTY, those spirits already prepackaged with an inborn gift which provided them with free thrills throughout their whole, livelong childhood day. When I think that as grownups they now float (they should have to walk?) about me, having undoubtedly inherited the earth and all that's in it, I must hold myself small. I tried. I practised. I punctiliously appreciated everything those little girls were said to appreciate in order to stimulate what I hoped were my merely dormant natural gifts. I posed breathlessly before sunsets. I sought casement windows (you try, in North Winnipeg) through which to hurl inspired phrases at the dawn. Useless. My stockings sagged. I did not walk in beauty. I was never to be one of those special people, the born elite of the world, with self-cleansing fingernails. Some of us are fated, again and again, to flunk boorishly the proferred moment. We flounder, instead, through a lifetime of staggering and unexpected encounters with the inappropriately exquisite. Go tell the world how haunted and baffled and thankful you can be for the illuminating beauty of an unbelievably dumb, tick-infested garbage scavenger of a failed racing greyhound. Why was Honey, in movement and in repose, the very stuff of loveliness? What are my standards? What do standards have to do with it? Standards mark the limits of yesterday's conquests. That dancer who soars and hangs an extra instant in the air, defeats time, transcends possibility, enlarges possibility, challenges the limitations of known dimension. Yesterday how was I to know that I could stand humbled and grateful before a phenomenally stupid, utterly blank-in-the brain creature of ineffable grace?

Why was it a joy to look at Honey, why do I still mentally strike matches and light candles to her?

> *You're wrong, auntie, she's not stupid!*
> *But Arnold, just look at her! We're talking about her, we're talking to her, we're looking at her, we're petting her. She's just so damn beautiful. But where is she? Look at her eyes, with what astonished rapture they gaze into each other across that deliciously modelled nose. Alone with her beloved!*
> *That doesn't mean she's stupid. She's the only dog I've ever known who has the sense to pick up her own mat and drag it back into the shelter of the porch when it begins to rain.*

Narcissus gazes at himself in the pool, on the brink of archetype, about to become the quintessential victim of aesthetics as real estate. Himself his own serpent, his own Eve, his own Adam reaching for his own apple and his own fall, precipitates his own foreclosure.

If we could learn to bear wonder we might never succumb to greed.

Beyond Narcissus, Honey wisely avoids the damp.

"Not dumb, auntie."

I stand corrected. Not dumb, for she has spoken to me of things to know and of ways of knowing that humble mere knowledge. My mother too has heard those voices in all her senses. For don't the eyes of this very dancing Senorita yearn toward each other with that same demure wonder and faintly comic intuition of her own being as revelation and fulfilment? It's funny how fond I am of those two Spanish dancers of mom's, though they always recall the pang of ancient but ever-renewable gaucherie. Perhaps it is because the created thing has been so intelligently conceived, and is so honestly and so joyfully recorded, that by opening myself and accepting their message, no matter how unexpected or even unwelcome, by responding to and accepting their validity in my reality, I am strengthened to accept myself too. I recognize that even my absurdities and humiliations are linked to some greater world of acceptance that is all of a piece with even my all-to-pieces.

I like your dolls, mama.
> *Good. Why else do you think I make them?*
Touché, old lady, here's mischief in your eye.

Never fear, she confides, *he'll sign. He's afraid. On my death-bed I'll threaten to take him with me. He'll be terrified. He'll sign then. And if that's not enough I'll threaten to come back and haunt him.* She glowers as daddy saunters by. *Afraid to endanger his precious little fur,* she growls. *Superstitious. He'll sign.*

I can tell that daddy knows that she is talking about him, and that she is not paying him compliments. But he's not sure of what she's saying, because at times like this he keeps on the move. Nevertheless he maintains a corner-of-the-eye aware-ness. His deafness has long since blunted his ability to slide accurately into a conversational topic already established. It has become his habit instead to launch himself on a stray word or phrase, heard or imagined, and swoop at an unexpected tangent into the conversation, where he will have his say on whatever biographically related topic is currently exercising him, though it may have taken place fifty or even 5,000 years ago, for as long as he can manage to hold the floor. Disconcerting though this can sometimes be to the unwary, it is not really an unfair tactic, when you consider that he sometimes waits days in utter silence for the opportunity. He has materialized, now, during a momentary pause, and launches into a defensive reminiscence in his own tumbled English.

This man come to me, it's how you call depression times, I got laid off from my good job, I got no work. He say to me, 'Vizeman, come work for me, lotsa work in my shop, I'm very busy, you get plenty overtime.'

Mama mutters counterpoint, *Oi, he's here already with the overtime.*

> *So I say, 'I want a paper, what you call it an agreement, it should be written down.' So he say 'What for you need it an agreement? I need you more than you need me.'*

> *Here comes the bad wife,* mutters mama.

> *And the woman,* daddy inclines his head slightly motherward, *she say to me, 'What you want? You got it to trust the man, Peisy!'*

> *You'll hear how I spoiled for him the business,* murmurs mama.

> *So I go work for him. I try. I'm a good worker, forst class tailor-forrier, no what you call it by me fonny business. Face in the needle. Forst week come for my pay I see what, no overtime? He say 'Overtime we pay it altogedder later.' All right, he say so, the woman say trust, okay.'*

> *Again the woman. What would he do without the woman? Without the woman he wouldn't even know how to make a fool of himself.*

> *Come eleven months, I been work hard, lots overtime. I not see my wife, my famly; leave house it's dark, come home kids asleep. I never knew my kids they grow up,* Daddy pauses a little wistfully, eyeing me.

> *True,* mama nods. *Emes, can't take away the truth.*

> *All of a sudden, how you say? The business is down. 'There's no work,' he tell me, 'I have to let you go.' All right, no work, what can I do? 'But where's my overtime?' He say, 'What overtime? Who say I owe you overtime? You got it proof I owe you overtime? Go sue me.' That he say, 'You got it proof I owe you overtime go sue me with lawyers.'* My dad stamps his foot, rocks to and fro and laughs ruefully.

'You got to trust, Peisy.' He throws my mother a glance and moves off, hands in pockets, secure that he has unassailably countered whatever accusations she might possibly have made against him.

> *So I trusted,* says mama. *My fault I trusted. He'll never forgive me I trusted. Who wants to live your whole life like you're surrounded by wild animals? Maybe we should have.*

My father has returned.

> *I try with the lawyers, but they're all how you say it, bought and sold. They take my few dollars on this side, he stuffs them in the pockets from behind, and they say, 'Vizeman, it's notting to do.'* Again he throws a glance, not unmixed with despair, and moves off.

> *That's what it's been like, my whole life he throws up to me,* says mama. *'You're so lucky!' people tell me. 'You live together like two little turtle doves.' Just because we don't fight in the streets; nobody has to know what goes on in the bedroom behind closed doors. That's one thing we agreed on from the start. If it so happened we disagreed, the children didn't have to suffer from it, their eyes should grow big over us, and we shouldn't become a freeshow for the neighbours, either. Nobody,* adds mama impressively, *has to know what I suffered behind that closed door.*

It is true that I was nearly twenty before I witnessed, for the first time, an open quarrel between my parents. And I was shocked, my eyes no doubt as large and darkly stunned as I remember my kid brother's were as we stood helpless witness, neophytes to the darker side of familiar things. Probably, it was so shattering an experience because we saw our parents for the first time as separate people, separate from us and from each other, with their own private grievances against each other, and were forced to comprehend that there were whole areas of their lives from which we had been excluded or spared. It was a wrench to learn how little I knew about what I thought I knew, a salutary wrench in the long run, to learn not to presume on the familiar, where sometimes the greatest mysteries reside.

I have often thought, since then, at what cost my parents tried to make of themselves a compensatory garden of possibility for us, in a world of disappointment and threat. What enormous efforts of understanding and control and tolerance they had to call up, to overcome incompatibilities and resentments, and to show us only respect and affection and loyalty. In later years they might sometimes mutter at each other, or flare up, each in his or her own highly sensitized cell of self. But how grateful I am now both that they spared us our childhood, and that they did finally, though not deliberately, quarrel furiously before us. It was a coming of age.

Of course I had always known that there were facts of life still missing. There was a part of me that said even then, during the great parental quarrel, "Ah, so that's it! How interesting! I wonder what else?" precisely as it had reacted to those other "facts of life" for which I had so patiently and so trustingly waited so long. For distressed though I may be, I must admit to an objective interest in the phenomena of life which usually acts as a safety valve in times of stress. Under emotional pressure, it provides a kind of layer in my internal atmosphere, which filters the intense rays of feeling at a certain angle, deflecting the heat of events, somewhat, and analysing their light. Artists, writers in particular, are sometimes accused of a lack of appropriate feeling when they respond in this way to significant events in their own lives. But surely a response which enables the making of public rainbows is a valid way of transforming the stuff of private scars.

So there was more than sex and the minty smell of oil-of-wintergreen from daddy's nightly·body rub behind that closed bedroom door! Of course. There are mysteries behind closed doors, and closed doors behind mysteries, behind which more mysteries lurk in prelude to more closed doors and further revelations. This I had discovered in my own nature though I had not been able to ascertain whether the closed door led to the mystery or the mystery led to the closed door, for sometimes, as scientific thinkers have pointed out, the answer presents itself readily; the problem is to find the question which makes sense of the answer. I usually know what is going to happen at the end of a story I write. The revelation, or series of revelations, for me, is in the hows and whys, which give the whole the relevance it has hopefully achieved by the time one has reached the "end." The name we give to the created thing, the "work," means not only that it is the result of someone's labour, but that it itself "works." It is, in a very important sense, alive. If you engage with it, it will work in you. The revelations of art are an attempt to capture the inner sense in the allusive suggestiveness of life, to penetrate its masks. We wrestle fragments of sensible form from flux, instants of inner sense from event, and if we're lucky, hallelujah, we've captured what? Little enough, it might seem, at most an instant in a fragment, but ALIVE, with its own separate, coherent vitality, its own resonance. And how it expands our own lives, if we allow it, our own consciousness of the possibilities of life! Creativity is an expression of vitality which strives for the enhancement of vitality.

My mother, when she begins to work, is often vague about what she is about to produce, and greets the creations of her own hands with exclamations of surprise. Nor is she rigid in defining her products.

   Here's a little cat for you.
 > Mama, does that look like a little cat to you?
 > All right, so it's a little pig.

When I sit down, with that familiar excitement, compounded of what? expectation? yes, and fear, to the typewriter, and my head is utterly blank though I've been preoccupied, obsessed with certain themes and events which can not occur until they make the right kind of emotional sense, I know it is revelations I'm waiting for, revelations which will arise from that mulch of confused fragments, those other hints and revelations, welcome and otherwise, with which life has already presented me. Most of us spend our lives tidying up unwanted feelings and contradictions and insights in the pursuit of the false ideal of antiseptic headspace. The artist, perhaps because of the intensity with which he has experienced them, knows that they contain vital energies to be harnessed, potent magic for the creation of worlds.

Advertizers, propagandists, demagogues, feeling-mongers of all sorts know how easy it is to arouse and lead people by playing on emotions and fears and directing stock responses to a predetermined end, which can be the relinquishment of personal responsibility and the surrender to mass manipulation. It is a temptation for those who understand the power and resource of a language to use it in this way, exploitively and with contempt for the audience it is so easy to manipulate. But by falsifying the perceptions and polluting the delicate streams of communication, they are cutting themselves off from both light and life, and banishing themselves to the limbo of their own making. Mind you, I've seen some beautifully appointed limbos.

The artist approaches his medium, rather, with passion and reverence, a state of mind which inclines toward responsibility and commitment. He knows that he is not simply master and manipulator of his language, ideally, but servant as well. He will use language not as a weapon with which to influence, tranquillize or control others, but as an instrument to create and explore analagous worlds and through them to try to comprehend himself and others.

How hard it is to be accurate. I have been writing much as though the whole process of creating something were some active, heroic struggle, Jacob wresting blessings from angels, Aristaeus seizing Proteus, engaging all the forms of form determined to fix, one after the other, and capture finally the ultimate form and matter of form and matter. That's so, that's the way it feels. But it is also other. For at the core of the process is the willingness to wait, to be patient, to drudge, to submit, to accept. It is a curious cast of mind and emotion, at once actively seeking and actively submitting, a state of strenuous passivity. Artists will sometimes even conceive of themselves as "instruments." In the case of writers I know this to be related not only to personal paranoia, but to that spooky feeling you get sometimes that you are both one who writes and who is being written with. It may at least partly explain why agnostics and even atheists may choose to serve their art with a faith and devotion usually considered appropriate only in the service of religion.

I am not, by the way, talking about automatic writing or the divine right of whatever happens to pop into your head to be taken down and enshrined as literature or art. For after all that I have described above, after all the prayer and the waiting and the drudgery, and even after the precious, riving instants of illumination, one must be willing to treat with that vicious little doubt, to be led back along small dishonesties through false insights over mires of padding to the central fault, under the crust of which the whole structure has perhaps already begun to rumble. And one must be willing to begin again. Research nowadays, I'm told, indicates that the critical-creative dichotomy is inherent in the very structural, bi-lobal, left-right functions of the brain itself; the binary nature of the human bind physically determined and limited; the struggles and conflicts, the periodic reversals of critical-creative ascendancy built in, predetermined in nature if not in instance. Wouldn't you just know it? And yet, perhaps it is at some optimal point of engagement of the apparently conflicting creative and critical modes and impulses that transformation occurs, old dimensions are breached, new realities created. Aren't inadequately conceived worlds, no matter how sincerely sweated over, well sacrificed in the service of the creation of the big bang, the expanding exhilaration of even one single metaphor which works?

In time I found that I was no longer nagging my mother as much as I used to; the years had begun to teach me to accept as well as to take, and to be content perforce with other than diagrammatic knowing. Still wistful for revelation I nevertheless took pleasure in familiarity with mystery, that continuing sensing that there is more here than I can quite comprehend or explain, which is in itself a kind of knowing. And my doll collection grew.

And these, says mama, turning from the suitcase while I'm still chuckling over the dolls she has already brought out, *are a couple of those children that are being born nowadays, you know, with the short arms and legs.*

Stunned, I stare at the limp, red and yellow mesh nylon onion sacking couple, each with its stumpy pair of knotted cord arms. For a moment, I am unable to speak. *You mean,* I utter finally, *thalidomide babies?*

My mother, watching me, says quickly, reassuringly, *But they grew up all right, you see they're dressed so nicely, all modern.*

Excited, obscurely triumphant, I know I have been given a key at last, but am as yet too astonished and fumble-headed to know how and indeed where to insert it. Several hours are to pass, and it is she who, finally, spurs me to a formulation of the question.

Mama walks purposefully to the dresser, picks up the thalidomide dolls. *I think I'll take these home.*

> *What?* To my surprise it comes out almost like a shout.

> *Because I could tell that you didn't like them.*

> *Oh no!* I cry. *Oh no! Oh no no no! Mama,* I blurt finally, reaching for the dolls. *I was just surprised. You always say you make the dolls to please the children and make them happy. Did you make these to please the children and make them happy too?*

Distressed, my mother tried to put into words at last what she had never realized I wanted to know.

> *It seems to me I see nature ... and I don't know how to explain it ... I feel if I'll make it that way the way nature gives it out ... any little thing it's got to be done, but I wouldn't give either an empty or unhappy things to young children.*
> *If, when it's a sad face or an ugly face that I know the people wouldn't look at them ... so I try to improve it ... I make a nice little mouth ... earrings ... eyes ... comes out a little more cheerful.*
> *It happens sometimes that I make them because I think of either a sick or unhappy person and I make it it should suit the purpose, but I wouldn't like to give it to the children when they don't look happy. I just either keep it in the house or ...*

I wish I could reproduce here what she told me in all its complexity; the tones of voice, the hesitations, the groping, the clarity of sense and emotion which emerged in spite of the barrier of speech, as mama tried to explain the confrontations and the mediations toward which she is impelled. It's not simply that she said things that I wanted to know, but that what she said changed the dimensions and the quality of my knowing. I have a recording of an interview I conducted with her then, because I knew I had to get her responses safely separate from the distortions of my memory of them, and perhaps of my interpretations too.

> *Why do you make them, mama?*
> *Because I see the sadness. I remember when I was a little child*

a tragedy in our town. The whole town gathered. They prayed and everything. A woman had to give birth to a child and she laboured all night and gave birth to a child with two heads, and I could never forget it. They put it on the window. Everyone came and saw the child. It was a tragedy I'll never forget. The woman never recovered her mind.

Well, it happened. It comes back to me and I like to see it again. It isn't pleasant. It's unpleasant but it reminds me of something that I saw and I don't like to see it, but it comes into my mind and I want to see it again. I don't know what drags me to it or what brings me to it. Like when I do the Siamese twins it reminds me of those children. I often think of twin sisters they should look alike . . . Siamese . . . undeveloped children.

I think of it and I hope life should improve and these things shouldn't happen because I hate to see life suffering . . .

Like I like to make people who are midgets, because I could see people they are midgets . . . and I like to create them the same as I see in nature—to express what I feel . . . what nature could bring out . . . the world should see that sometimes there is tragic in families that it's hard to bear.

I remember we had a governor in our town. He had grown-up children who were students. They were brilliant. But the youngest, the governess used to take it to the park.

I loved that child. Its body was like a twelve month old, but it had water in its head. Its head was like the biggest watermelon. It didn't smile or talk. Its head must have bothered it. He looked like a sick person. I thought if I gave it a little love when I was near it it would feel better.

So I try to bring back the child because I pitied it and I loved it. I try to create that little head, too, all perfect. I don't know, I loved it. To give it life again, it's unpleasant but you see these creatures.

And it reminds me. Nature gives it out. Something is in it and it reminds me and I try to create the same thing, to see something

that I went through it ... as a youngster, but it still comes back
to me. It brings back memories. I saw life and I went through
it. I don't want to say it makes me happy, but I want to see it
again. It's like a dream.
Like for instance I saw once a cow had two? three heads I
think. It reminds me. Nature gives it out ... there must be
something in it ... and I want to see it.
I hope it would improve, and there shouldn't be crippled chil-
dren, there shouldn't be children suffering.

So mama's work, whatever its ostensible purpose, is also an expression of her profound need to engage with life in those areas which have most moved her, a need so compelling that it has transformed her craft to the language of that need's fulfilment. It is a complex need, not only to recreate and record and celebrate those things in life which have brought her joy, but to come to terms with, to make bearable in the process of confrontation and recreation, those realities which have given pain. She spends her creative energies plotting strategies to this end, though of course confrontation, mediation and presentation are all one gesture to her, all encompassed in the act of "making."

Even the most apparently simple work is a complex organization, performing simultaneously a number of functions. Consider, for instance, that the maker not only creates the work, he creates in the audience, through the work, the desire to and the possibility of being able to confront and experience optimally its revelations without being damaged or alienated by them. Not surprisingly, words so often used in describing human-created things are words of multiple connotation like "design," which implies not only planning and harmonious relationships and shapeliness as basic functional as well as aesthetic characteristics of the work (a poor design doesn't "work"), but an object to be achieved by the work itself, a "design" on the part of the artist. I have noticed that great works of literary art, those which arouse in reader or viewer the "tragic emotion," face simultaneously inwards, making what happens to the protagonist real and inescapable, and outwards, building in the audience step by step the strength to face what is happening to the characters, to absorb the awesome life-giving emotional comprehension offered, of what is potential to all humanity, and to share in the sense of dignity and acceptance which the experience confers. Something happens in the work, but something also happens crucially in the audience.

Every creator must find his own "art," his own way of discovering what he knows to himself and his audience, of revealing his truths as simultaneously inevitable and bearable. This is a process at the opposite end of experience from the reductive, mass hysterical immolation and acceptance achieved by the exploitive use of language and people. For it heightens, rather than diminishes, the individual awareness. It therefore does not exclude the possibility that those whose vitality and comprehension have been extended through the working of an artistic experience in them, might thereafter take a greater interest in and responsibility for real problems which have not previously been quite so real to them. Art as a way of knowing can stimulate the thinking and feeling processes. The audience member may be aroused to examine, weigh, extrapolate and extend ideas and feelings for himself. That's part of the potential educative function of art, and what is so terrifying to people who are afraid some "unacceptable" aspect of reality might be acknowledged this way.

So mama mediates, coaxing and soothing herself and us out of our fear and pain, out of superstitious and superficially aesthetic recoil. She makes, in her creations, bridges to lead us to new territories of the heart, to more generous comprehension, to wholer and more satisfying aesthetic. Each junk and button picture, every little doll is an expression of what it's really like "to be," a submission to, a reconciliation with, an acceptance and a celebration of being.

I had known all along that mama was using biographical material in her work. Now it became clear that the past is not simply a mine where experiential data is stored, to be brought out and used at will, but a minefield of unresolved energies, dynamic, exerting pressure for release, vital trace "experiences" surfacing obsessively again and again to demand direct or parallel expression, seeking some form of recognition in being, some shape and at least temporarily satisfying completion. From here can come any or all of impulse, theme or subject for a "work." Into mama's works flow not only what she has clearly perceived, and what life has taught her, but also the living, unresolved, the still working metaphors of her personal history.

From mama's words, too, I realized even more sharply than hitherto how certain obsessively recurring ideas can be formed in a person's mind; indeed, how they can help to determine the very cast and colouration of that mind, providing, for instance, the key metaphors and analogies by which an artist may attempt, again and again, to interpret the very nature of existence. How often and in what a variety of physical and emotional contexts did the enigmas of duality and fragmentation within the whole present themselves to my mother when she was yet a child. How visibly, palpably concrete were the correspondences she encountered everywhere; how impressive and frightening and far-reaching their power of emotional evocation. That two-headed infant in the window, prayed for by the whole town, with the labouring mother who never recovered her mind, that three-headed calf, that melon-headed baby of the rich and brilliant family, bursting with the divisive waters within, are images which repeat, reinforcing each other, etching deeply parameters of pathos and horror in nature. They mark the out-lines of an experience of existence. And what of the in-lines? What of that river which flowed daily through her life — two rivers or one? — flowing towards each other, coming together around a small pleasure island, then flowing through the town as one, and yet in two different channels, one blue, one silvery gray, separating to surround the island town of Bogopol, and thereafter to flow off, each river in its separate direction once again. This was the river, these were the rivers where she skated in terror and high glee, where people had ice fights and built beautiful crèches and drowned, where she bathed and fetched water and the postman exposed himself; she strolled across its bridges and her dog was savaged here, the river in which "some pee, some drink," around which her triple towns had grown, on one arm of which her future husband's hamlet lay. She sees and fondly describes that river still as "like sisters, one with brown hair and one with red, or like Siamese twins." I have spoken of the out-lines and the in-lines. Of the within-lines, that private territory of my mother's inner being, even I will not presume to speak. Suffice that we can see so clearly and repeatedly elsewhere the lineaments of her vision.

Apparently, through repetition and multiple reinforcement, some classes of event can groove themselves indelibly into the human psyche, till they become key symbols of basic qualities of existence. Those "living" traces, those "more-than-memories" which dominate the inner felt-world, continue to work away in us, digesting new experience according to a multi-dimensioned logic of their own. Even apparently dissimilar experiences are analysed, related and recombined by a kind of flexible, vital analogical system, according to their emotional weight, their shape, their density, the similarity of sense elements, the suggestiveness of their echoes, the pitch of their resonance, the accident of their having occurred simultaneously, or at a particular emotional temperature, or through whatever connections and correspondences and paths, and even transformations, they can be brought to make the arcane "sense" which dominates within. We are wistfully attached to the idea of "reason," of a logically sequential, consciously controlled linear existence in time. It is, of course, an illusion. We end up selecting, mysteriously, again and again, in whatever disguise, the emotional shape of the world in which we were first moulded.

Again and again my mother has explored in her creations those mysteries of multiplicity, of fragmentation in unity, one-in-two and two-in-one, has tried to reconcile visually the implied frustrations of tied separate beings, of fragmented wholes. She "sees" these things. They look out at her from the most unexpected places. My niece has a delicate piece of fan-shaped coral, in pattern reminiscent of a human brain. On it my mother has sewn two sets of human features, peering out. Recently, she sewed two of her crocheted rag potholders together and produced her first two-faced hand puppet, which has of course been followed by a whole series of variations and developments. One person wearing two of these puppets can, simply by turning his hands, enact a four-person scene. Two children can do a play with eight characters.

Often, a doll will have two different coloured eyes, and not by accident.

> *I saw once a boy, for the first time in my life; he was a cousin who came to apprentice with my father at his Bar Mitzvah and stayed till he was married, and he had one brown eye and one eye that was half brown and half green, straight up and down one half of his eye was green, one half brown. One eye. I marvelled.*

Just this morning when I was thinking of my mother's way of describing the two-one-two rivers, I saw them briefly as a human body spreadeagled, with a teeming town, its head, at one fork, and a pleasure island, its crotch, at the other; its nature human, binary, unified and bifurcated, held together, pulling apart, coming from all directions and flowing in all directions, concentrating life around itself. She could have been describing herself, or indeed, as I believe she would herself understand, us all.

The receptive-expressive creative person seems to concentrate in himself and focus, in his work, currents from the shared emotional and intellectual life of his society. His product epitomizes, and in some form projects resolutions for, underlying dilemmas of the human in general and his culture in particular. By resolutions I do not mean that the creator necessarily solves problems in any practical final sense, but that he resolves them in terms of the situation in which he has embodied them. He works through a problem by presenting it and exploring it in action. The work is a revelation of its nature, an exploration of its implications, a venting of its emotional potential, rather than a solution in any practical sense, since often what he is driven to explore is the structure of enigma, the heart of the insoluble. Those unresolved energies of which I have spoken exist, under varying degrees of pressure, in all of us. They are potent with the need to grow in some extra-cerebral space, give shape to themselves, release their emotional loads, and function in some sensibly tangible form. Creating is a way of growing. The artist undertakes an organized expression, "the growth" of some of this seething potential. Ideally, his performance is both a personal and a social act.

It is always dangerous to block growth. Lacking appropriate outlet, those energies will sometimes leak their juice through unexpected conductors, into our daily lives, and manage to fictionalize some aspect of the lives of even the most rational. For the emotionally impelled imagination neither scorns nor can be contained by the unilinear reasoning to which we think we are clinging as we grope our way along time. It travels, being in every sense "quicker" than the "I," by all the real magic routes of the underground. Transformed, disguised, translated, metamorphosed, connection-hopping, intuition-leaping, instantaneously empire-building, fragmenting and reshaping language itself, it will commandeer even the humblest sound, syllable, the merest nuance, to make its connections. Subject neither to restrictions of time, place, nor other normally accepted dimension, it can feed into our lines of reasoning, making the kind of sense which will drive us with impeccable logic, utter conviction, and passionate emotion right up the wall, where we discharge by madly acting out our distorted visions. Not only individuals, but whole societies have succumbed to this destructive potential in our own day. For growth can be distorted. It is not necessarily moral or creative in itself.

The language of speech is such a superb medium, the very words we use are so freighted with emotional coloration and meanings, with imagery and symbol, that the process of stringing words together is also a process of suppressing and trimming away unwanted connotations so that we can communicate only what we think we want to communicate. But the inner needs are "quicker." We think we want to say one thing but the very words we use and the way they suddenly come together out of our own mouths, can subvert our plans. We release all kinds of explosions, echoes, unintended confessions, cries and admissions in even the simplest things we choose to say, the very tones and modulations of the saying. Let me give a small example, familiar in kind to us all. The other day I was explaining to my husband that my sister had a new job in which she had to remove the genitalia of crickets for biochemical analysis. What I actually said, with great relish and enthusiasm, was "You know what she's going to be doing? Cutting the balls off critics!" To which he replied thoughtfully, "If she can find them."

The "work," therefore, is also a way of attracting and relatively harmlessly discharging related unresolved energies in the perceiver; the more receptive the audience, the better the connection, the profounder and more gratifying the effect. When the artist is functioning in a closely integrated society he may become a kind of oracle of the very spirit of his culture, expressing its inner and its outer being in all its density and complexity, to reveal the society to itself, and to make it also accessible to others. After all my half-joking but dead serious speculation about the curiously beautiful and evocative effect of partly crossed eyes (eyes which gaze in opposite or asymmetrical directions also have distinct effects) I finally found, not long ago, two Japanese wood carvings, figures of women, one holding a lotus, and one a jewel. Their eyes gaze with profound tranquillity, along lines which must surely meet just beyond if not actually right through their noses, where they encounter the most ineffable of in-sights. I know they are really gazing right through and into the depths of the eye-I-aye itself, into themselves and beyond, to the very core of being. I am told that they are Arahats, Buddhist saints who have reached the gates of heaven but of their own accord have chosen not to take the final step, but to return to work with and for humanity. Without knowing much at all about the religion whose preferred perceptions these figures help to express and not knowing who they were when I picked them up, I nevertheless recognized them in a language I can know in spite of my ignorance of the formal reasonings of Buddhism. The language of the carvings is available to me.

There are many languages in China, and people from one district have difficulty in communicating with people from areas nearby. But they all share the same written picture language, so that if you can read and write Chinese, or the old Japanese, you can communicate though you may not be able to exchange agreed-upon sound constellations. So too with those insights which are available to all humanity, though not equally valued in each culture; the artist can make them trans-culturally available to succour even a foreigner's need.

To me these figures are a source of inexpressible comfort and peace. Together with my monkey god, a figure from the Chinese Buddhist pantheon, a symbol, apparently, of the ungovernable imagination finally under some positive direction and control, they speak to me. I have been discussing the reinforcement of image, of correspondences and the magnetic power of metaphor and analogy. Now I can tell the family secret which has, in a sense, governed my life. When my mother was pregnant with me, she went to see a film called *Monkey Talks*, in which Lon Chaney played a man who plays a monkey in a cage in a circus. He is dressed, of course, in a monkey costume. And he falls in love with a girl who scorns him because he looks like a monkey. Who knows, maybe she prefers the bear. Anyway, my mother was disturbed by the film and came away remembering an old superstition that if you became deeply affected by some being or image during your pregnancy, your child would be born in the image which had disturbed you. For the rest of her pregnancy she worried that I was going to resemble a monkey. First thing she asked the doctor, "Is it normal?"—I think, because she was too embarrassed to ask "Is it human?" That, in spite of, and perhaps because of the accompanying assurances by herself and sundry witnesses, that I was an unusually beautiful baby, has been the governing anecdote of my existence. When I ran across the book *Monkey*, translated from the Chinese, it was an encounter of recognition. Years later I recognized my totem, a gilded wooden monkey in an antique shop in Winnipeg (whose eyes, by the way, gaze somewhat asymmetrically outward), and I marked numerous essays to earn the money to rescue him.

At some point in his or her career nearly every actively creative person is forced to confront the limitations of his medium, for language too can be a false god.

Mom is in her seventy-eighth year. We have just discovered that she has cancer. She has rejected drastic remedies. Her doctors in Canada are humane, and have allowed her the dignity of choice.

It's in nature, she tries to reassure me. *Child we must accept what is in nature.*

I telephone frequently. *So far everything is fine,* she tells me. *If my boarder will only stay in his room, and not try to take over the whole house, I would be content.*

She lives in remarkable symbiosis with her tumor, writes her doctor.

While the sun shines, I want to live, she remarks. Trips and visits continue.

I feel the need to cling. *I wish you'd make me a big picture, something out of your life.*
It's funny, I was thinking all last night about my father. How hard he worked. Physically. Every time he raised that big hammer over his head, mama illustrates with both arms, *I used to get a spasm in my heart because he worked so hard. I thought I'd make a picture of him, hammering those spokes. And my mother, bringing his lunch.* Thoughtfully, *I'll have to look, when I get home, to see if I have jewellery and buttons.* But when I mention the project again a few days later she tells me, *I just can't bear to think of my father as little buttons and rags.*

During the Second Great World War, when the Ukraine was about to be overrun by the Germans, the Russians began to evacuate their target civilian population, the Jews. My mother's father at first refused to leave his lifelong home. Perhaps he remembered those gentlemanly young Austrian officers of the First World War, those my mother used to tell me about, who, as prisoners of war had had the freedom of the town, and had danced away the nights with his young daughters. From such men what was there to fear? Strangers had invaded Russia before. They passed. Russia remained. But he was finally persuaded, and my grandparents and aunts and their families loaded what they could onto wagons and joined the caravan of evacuees. Not knowing where or when the journey might end, but having been through wars and revolutions and famines and plagues, my grandfather made sure that they would have the wherewithal to feed themselves. He tied his cow and her calf to the wagon. They had not gone far when the calf broke loose, and bolted homeward. Grandfather set out to catch her, and was never seen by his family again. Years later, my aunts were told that the old man had found his way back to the town eventually, and had been trapped there by the invading forces. For a while he survived by begging food from his old neighbours. German-allied Roumanian soldiers entered the town first, and curiously, in spite of their known ferocity toward the Jews, they left the bearded old man alone. But when the Germans arrived they relieved him swiftly and finally of his illusions.

My grandmother too left the family group when grandfather failed to return. Never having been separated from him since their marriage in another century, she wandered from junction to junction in search of him, until she too was scooped up by the Germans, my beautiful grandmother I had always been so flattered to hear I might resemble when I grew up, and dumped in a slave labour camp, where she too perished. My uncle Sander died fighting in the seige of Sebastopol, and my aunt Chana's husband also died in battle. My cousin Isaac, Aunt Rose's son, the babe my Winnipeg Aunt Sonia held in her arms when she was a young girl, who aroused in her such a passion of love that many many years later she confided in me that she was returning to Russia for a visit mainly to see him again, also fought in the war, and wears his medal permanently, a plate embedded in his forehead to replace the bone.

I have been reading to mama the beginning of my book on her

dolls. Friends arrive, and mama says challengingly, *Have you read them what you're writing about your mother?* as though daring me to reveal my infamy.

You should see, she tells them, *how a daughter treats a mother.*

I read. When I am done, *You see,* says mama, *how she makes fond of me?*

At the outburst of laughter she looks from one to the other uncertainly.

Fon ... fond ... I say right?

As usual, mama, more right than you know.

My father's comments on current personal affairs are usually confined, nowadays, to brief but often reiterated questions or statements about whatever makes him anxious enough, or briefly gladdens his heart enough, to disturb his habitual reverie.

Where's the child? Where's Dmitry? All members of his family must be accounted for at the appropriate times.

They haven't sent my cheque yet, or, with brimming joy, *They've raised me ten cents this month!* Economic anxiety remains deeply ingrained.

Will you phone the hospital? I'm running out of heart pills. The panic sets in weeks ahead of the likelihood.

On the departure of a guest to whom he has been hospitably revealing some portion of his life's saga for as long as he's been able to manage, he may go so far as to ask, genially, *Who was that person?*

No wonder his brief account of the morning my mother broke her hip, felt like a torrent.

OOdl, now I can tell you. I had such a fright. I awoke one morning and I couldn't find your mother. I went from room to room, bedroom, bathroom, kitchen, all over the house, and she wasn't there. I didn't know where she was. Then Arnold told me she had fallen and they had taken her away to the hospital while I slept. She didn't want to wake me, so she went by herself to the bathroom and she fell. I didn't even hear her calling.

Recovered, now, from his short period of heart failure, he follows after her walker, vigilant, he who as a young man a-courting had been told that for sure he wouldn't know how to hold this girl's parasol properly, still claiming his bride from the yawning future.

Mama, I have hesitated to ask. *You haven't mentioned that paper for a long time. Do you still want daddy to sign?*
Mama bursts into gleeful laughter. *Didn't I tell you? He signed. About three years ago I got him to sign. I fooled him.* Mama glances toward daddy triumphantly. He still moves ceaselessly about the house, though with shuffling tread, and his song is fainter. Sometimes I have to pause to listen for it, though *Zedah's singing in the bathtub,* his granddaughter reports cheerfully of his Friday morning bath.
I told him it was a paper from the doctor, says mama. *So he signed.* Crafty as Ulysses, having re-established sovereignty over her remains, mama chuckles.

She too has recovered from that day when I returned from the hospital without him, and I opened the front door to see her scuttling frantically away behind her walker, with head averted so I shouldn't see the red face and the welling eyes. "He wants so much to live," she told me later.

No one can prevent those moments of panic, or shore up each instant against breakthrough of tidal anguish. But it is wasteful to pre-mourn. So we celebrate every day, for life still flows strongly in fragile vessels. "I'm fighting cancer, you know," I heard mother tell a guest composedly. Always a living barometer, she is even more sensitized now. Her body, attuned to the earth's minutest seasons, forefeels the slightest change, and sleeps it into being. She awakes, adjusted. "You see, I told you a change was coming. Now I'm all right." And she addresses herself to projects in hand.

We have celebrated her 81st birthday, and their 58th wedding anniversary, for mama was married on her birthday.

Unable to sleep as late as usual, excited because she is expecting her grandson from Florida, she rises, washes thoroughly, and appears, fresh and young behind her clicking walker, where I sit working in the kitchen. She takes the green-eyed doll from the cork board, together with her mate, and clicks off to the front porch. She has, during the short time she has been here, amassed an amazing number of derelict objects, keeping them in piled-up cardboard tissue boxes and paper bags beside her, against the wall on her bed. She occupies little space herself. One day, while she was still bedridden, I brought her a button I had found. *Into the secret treasure box!* she sang, and popped it into one of her tissue cartons. On the porch I remind her it is her birthday.

And my wedding day. Today my mother is groaning in childbirth; I am preparing for the mikvah. I didn't believe in those things but I wanted to please them all. My aunt had the honour of escorting me to the bath. What other bride still showed her first night's sheets to her mother-in-law? It was laughable but I did it. I wanted to satisfy them all, my aunt who was afraid I might be an old maid, my mother-in-law that her son had chosen well, my parents. I was a good child that way. I tried to please them and it didn't hurt me any.

And yet I felt exactly then about these things as you young people feel nowadays.

As she speaks mama is rapidly effecting a sex change, transforming the green-eyed girl to a green-eyed man. For days the doll has bothered her. *I could see a more intelligent girl than those foolish green eyes show.* She has made another girl, with blue sequin sparkling eyes. Now she ties back the blonde hair of the original, adds looping brown whiskers, and exchanges the delicate copper button for a larger, more assertive button nose. She sews the smaller button on the female, a finer feature, consistent with her greater delicacy.

You see? The green, foolish eyes fit better here than for a girl.
> *Do you feel that foolish green eyes are more appropriate to a man?*
> *No. That's where I saw them.*

Precise observation is not allowed to slop over into generalized judgment so easily. Simple honesty and a lively critical intelligence monitor and reject any such temptation to distort. Would that more "serious" artists, and yes indeed more critics, were so finely attuned to the real note.

Let me here forestall one such generalization. I do not mean to imply, in what I have written, that all creative people have either the same temperament or attitudes or world view or morality or kinds of insight or intelligence which I have ascribed to my mother. I do not even believe that creativity and morality are necessarily always harness mates, though for me this has been a bitter reality to have to accept. One has only to look at the mad scientist so popular in fiction and film, to realize that society too recognizes and fears the possibilities of creativity run amok, of Monkey stealing and eating all the peaches of eternal life, of the original intelligence set to destructive ends, unguided by morality or responsiblity. And aside from specific evil intent, there is the real fact of conflicting moralities. There is the real fact of creativity in the service of destruction, of destruction passionately believed in as means to "higher" creativity. Like any human tool creativity can, paradoxically, be destructive. It can be misused. It is human. We do not have to accept all the worlds we can comprehend, but it makes good sense to stretch our comprehension to encompass even those which give us little pleasure. It's good to know what's out there. As a Jew I know only too well by how many different sets of ground rules the same game can be simultaneously played by everyone else. I have learned that not only the ground rules but the game itself can be shifted on you without notice, and indeed without conscious recognition on the part of some of the shifting players. I have seen my own role spelled out in art often enough to know that I am trapped in many an impurely conceived fictitious world which will help to perpetuate the abominable fictions of the real world in which I must daily function. I recognize that our created worlds echo also our own limitations of comprehension, our own vested emotional as well as other interests. And I know that there are created worlds to which we will not give the recognition necessary to existence, even in art, because we cannot cope with their implications. It is important to know all this, because it happens to be true, but life is too interesting to waste in bewailing it. To survive and flourish in a world in which you're held in multiple bind is existential virtuosity. To succeed in enlarging the possibilities of that world in even the smallest degree would indeed be mastery, the worthy dream of any hopeful artist.

Nothing holds still. My father's footsteps once paced and skipped and stamped; they strolled and walked; eventually they shuffled; and suddenly they drag. One day he looked at me, from the chair in which he sat shrunken, close to the living room heating pipes, and in his glance was an embarrassed, appealing, almost apologetic expression which dared me to confirm that he was failing. Not long afterwards, while I was still hoping that I had not comprehended, I happened to turn from the stove, and met in his eyes a new and chilling expression: speculative, objective, distant; almost . . . indifferent?

Now I sit facing him in the hospital again. Every day I try to save up things to tell him, but my news is quickly exhausted, and we are silent much of the time. Sometimes I feel his eyes on me, when I am looking elsewhere, and when he looks away I am compelled to inspect him repeatedly, furtively.
Occasionally, he launches on a familiar story-sequence from his past, and once or twice I have been jarred when he mistook me for someone else in that past. But only briefly. Each time I have been able, quickly, to re-establish our connection without embarrassing him too much. And we have lapsed again into silence. It is an extension of the silence of years. What can I do about it now?
What people are! Daddy breaks suddenly into animated speech. *My uncle, the one who taught me to sew, you know the rich one; of his sons the cleverest was a fragile boy. He became sick with some kind of stomach ailment. He couldn't contain his bowels. He couldn't help it. He was very ill. But because he didn't hold it in his father beat him and beat him and beat him, right there in his bed, sick as he was.* My father shudders, his eyes the huge, intense eyes of a wounded child. *Finally, the boy cried out, 'Father, let's make up, I won't live much longer!' And in a little while he died.*
What people are, whispers my 84-year-old, dying father.

It was a story he'd never told me before, nor had my mother heard it, in all their years together. Neither did he speak of the beatings he himself must have received, when, at nine, he came, a proud but puny boy, into his uncle's power. There was something awesome in his choice of silences.

The shock has been great for mother. She had always expected to precede him, and now, to her own slow ordeal has been added the burden of her husband's absence. She tries to wake earlier in the day, and tire herself out, because the long nights have become terrible. And yet her spirit has rallied, "for the time I have left." I even overheard her joking about my father's current situation with her "new granddaughter," the bride her eldest grandson had brought to get to know her. "Adele says he's surrounded by old ladies there. Well, I've never been jealous." Nevertheless she's changed her mind about cremation, though not about her post-mortem medical connection. The co-habits of nearly fifty-nine years are hard to break. "Why should he lie there alone with all those blondes?" Eventually, her bits and pieces will lie beside her husband's remains. She has already ordered the double tombstone with the hearts and clasped hands which her small granddaughter helped design at her request. To a question from the monument maker, she replied, "I don't know. I have no experience. I've never died before."

I feel that my body is beginning to give in, she told me recently. At the clinic her Dr. noticed that she has indeed lost ground since her last examination. *My friend is dead,* she explained to him.

As my editor went out the door, she turned, hand moving to hip, and remarked, *It's funny how I come alive when a young man's around.*

My daughter's little friend was waiting on the porch when I brought her home from school the other day. *I've just been talking to your bobba. She's so interesting! Bobba Waisman is so interesting to talk to!*

What were you talking about that was so interesting? I asked mom later.
> *Oh, she told me all about herself, practically from the moment she arrived in the world. And we discussed.*

Ever so diminutive now, tomorrow she will be 82. She pauses as she labours, determinedly unaided, toiling up the outdoor steps. *Life is so strange. Look how as I grow lighter, I grow heavier.*

As for the fact that she may yet have to suffer great pain, she would prefer not to. *But then, how am I better than others?*

I have tried to present my mother within her contexts, to re-create the feel of her particularity, her unique self within its unique world. I have tried to give some feeling, too, of the ambience of the world which she has helped to create for the selves most closely impinging on her. I have tried also to examine her functioning within the particular context of her chosen and fated language of expression, in the hope of helping to make the potential pleasure to be got from her work more available to those to whom it is unfamiliar. And I have attempted to isolate and examine in her and her work at work, some of the motivating factors and salient characteristics of the creative impulse and creative process in general, in the hope of contributing something to the understanding of an as-yet imperfectly understood and frequently repressed human function which I believe to be vital to human well-being. I do not believe, as some artists do, that understanding more about the whys and hows of creative activity will make the magic go away. Mystification is a parody of the wonder of mystery. It has a legitimate comic function of sorts, and is a useful tool in the service of elite and partisan interests that have little to do with the act of creation itself. But I cannot believe that the high mystery to which I address myself will go twittering off forever like the fairies at the bottom of my garden, at the mere approach of my clunking tread. Far more sensibly it will tease me on and on, letting my inadequacies set their own limits, allowing me to earn my own insights. In our age an hysterical human tendency has more than once chosen to equate solution with destruction. It is also possible to choose to equate solution with an enlargement of understanding, and the opening of further paths for exploration. Therefore it is my hope that a little pragmatic elucidation, a little demystification, will not banish the glamour of mystery from art, but rather make it even more available. It's always worked that way for me. Each time, the end of the process which has promised to flush out and fix reality is also the end of the illusion that I can do it once and for all. What would I do, I wonder, if it weren't? What is EUREKA anyway? Perhaps that is why the end of a project, so ardently pursued, is so often the beginning of a period of depression, an awareness of limitation, from which the only escape is, eventually, a re-entry into process, the further extension of my own particular mode of creation. For me that is where engagement will always lie, and the pleasure is in the engaging.

Thankfully, I have mom's dolls to remind me of the true function of art as one of life's few great gifts that is undiminished in the sharing. They are not made to be bought or sold. In terms of the artistic market place they are value-less. They are simply, briefly here, like the rest of us. They are all about being alive. Their very existence suggests that human creativity and its products, in many forms, could be increased multifold, could even, oh heresy! flood the market, be within reach of all human beings, whether as creators or as recipients of the true, free gift, the proferred gift from one human being to others, of an enlarged existence. Because it is a real existence, we must experience it; we must be willing to receive. The pain of growth as well as its pleasures are involved, the rigours of judgment too. We must be fully alive to meet the challenge of yet more life. Perhaps that is why we resist, and allow our potential talents to be so easily taken from us and from our children. It is the emotional, not the financial expenditure we are afraid we cannot afford. We see the emotional expenditure demanded as loss, the transformation or enlargement offered as potential destruction; thus we deny ourselves the investments with the greatest growth potential that life is likely to bring us. And then, because we feel obscurely cheated, we cry out, "Is this all that life has to offer?"

Attitude is a catching thing. I remember one of mom's little foster granddaughters bringing her a bottle doll, a queen, lovingly made, and tendered with the comment, "Bobba Waisman always gives away her dolls. Someone should give her a doll too."

As my mother's daughter I am impelled to try to re-create for you some sense of what I have learned from what I know of her life, from her words, and from the products of her hands. I am duty bound to share my luck, lest I too find myself, on the brink of some tired and companionable dawn, facing the gentle query, "And what are you doing for the community?"

Well then, mother and her works have taught me about

ART AS COMMUNICATION
ART AS IMITATION
ART AS MEDIATION
ART AS REORGANIZATION
ART AS RE-CREATION
ART AS INTEGRATION
ART AS INNOVATION
ART AS INTERPRETATION
ART AS RECONCILIATION
ART, above all, as CELEBRATION.

And more, mama and her work have confirmed in me the knowledge that art, uncapitalized and unshunned, is our human birthright, the extraordinary right and privilege to share, both as givers and receivers, in the work of continuous creation. Understanding this, the questioner may no longer have to ask the abysmal, "Is this all there is to life?" Instead, restored in innocence and wonder, he may be able to exclaim with me, as I watch my mother's hands still at work as I type this now, "All this? Oh mother! And yet more?"

Obviously, this book is about me too, about why I write and about my sources and my roots and the complexities of identity. It's true, the thought has more than once occurred to me, that in that last moment, as I lie dying, my mother's life will flash before my eyes.

I wonder if it will be my version?

By the same author

THE SACRIFICE
CRACKPOT

Canadian Cataloguing in Publication Data

Wiseman, Adele, 1928-
    Old woman at play

ISBN 0-7720-1230-X

1. Wiseman, Chaika, 1896-   2. Dollmakers —
Canada — Biography. I. Title.

TT175. W58W57   745.59'22   C78-001364-6

Photography by TOM TSUJI.

© 1978 Adele Wiseman

ISBN 0-7720-1230-X

Printed in Canada